# OHIO DAY TRIPS

CATHY HESTER SECKMAN

## DEDICATION

For Andrea and Larry Adkins, wishing them great day trips.

## ACKNOWLEDGMENTS

For help with photos and information, thanks go to Beth Santore, Warren Hyer, Robin Webster, Brent Haynes, Carolyn and Frank Sipkovsky, Lana Grim, and LCDR Jon Benvenuto, USCG.

**Safety Note** Ohio is home to a variety of potentially dangerous animals, including venomous snakes and scorpions, as well as natural hazards, such as temperature extremes, sudden flash floods, and cliffs and dropoffs. Always heed posted safety warnings, take common-sense safety precautions, and remain aware of your surroundings. You're responsible for your own safety.

Editor: Andrew Mollenkof
Cover and book design: Hilary Harkness
Proofreader: Emily Beaumont
Typography: Karla Linder
Maps: Steve Jones
Indexer: Potomac Indexing, LLC
Front cover photos: Ashtabula harbor light: Wirestock Creators/shutterstock.com; asphalt: Irina Gutyryak/shutterstock.com; guitar: Burbuzin/shutterstock.com
Back cover photos: Hocking Hills waterfall: Kenneth Keifer/shutterstock.com; Rock & Roll Hall of Fame: Henryk Sadura/shutterstock
Photo credits on page 183
ADK branding background on page 184 by chyworks/Shutterstock.com

10 9 8 7 6 5 4 3 2
**Ohio Day Trips by Theme**
First Edition 2018, Second Edition 2025

Published by Adventure Publications
An imprint of AdventureKEEN
310 Garfield Street South
Cambridge, Minnesota 55008
(800) 678-7006
adventurepublications.net

Printed in China
LCCN 2024060760 (print); 2024060761 (ebook)
ISBN 978-1-64755-480-4 (pbk.); ISBN 978-1-64755-481-1 (ebook)

# OHIO DAY TRIPS

CATHY HESTER SECKMAN

Adventure Publications
an imprint of AdventureKEEN

# MAP 1

## WESTERN OHIO

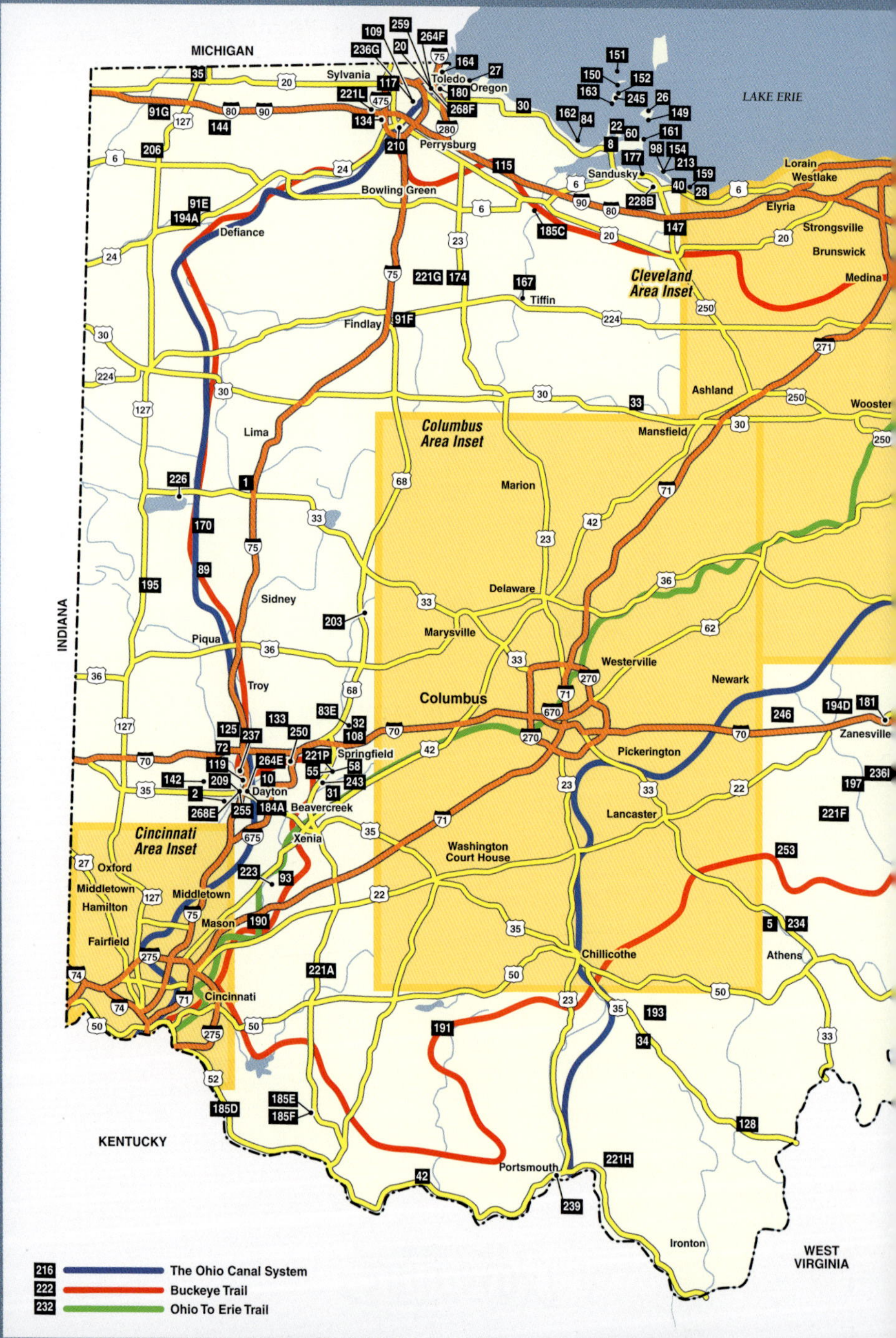

# CONTENTS

MAP 1 MAP 2 MAP 3 MAP 4 MAP 5

# MAP 2

## EASTERN OHIO

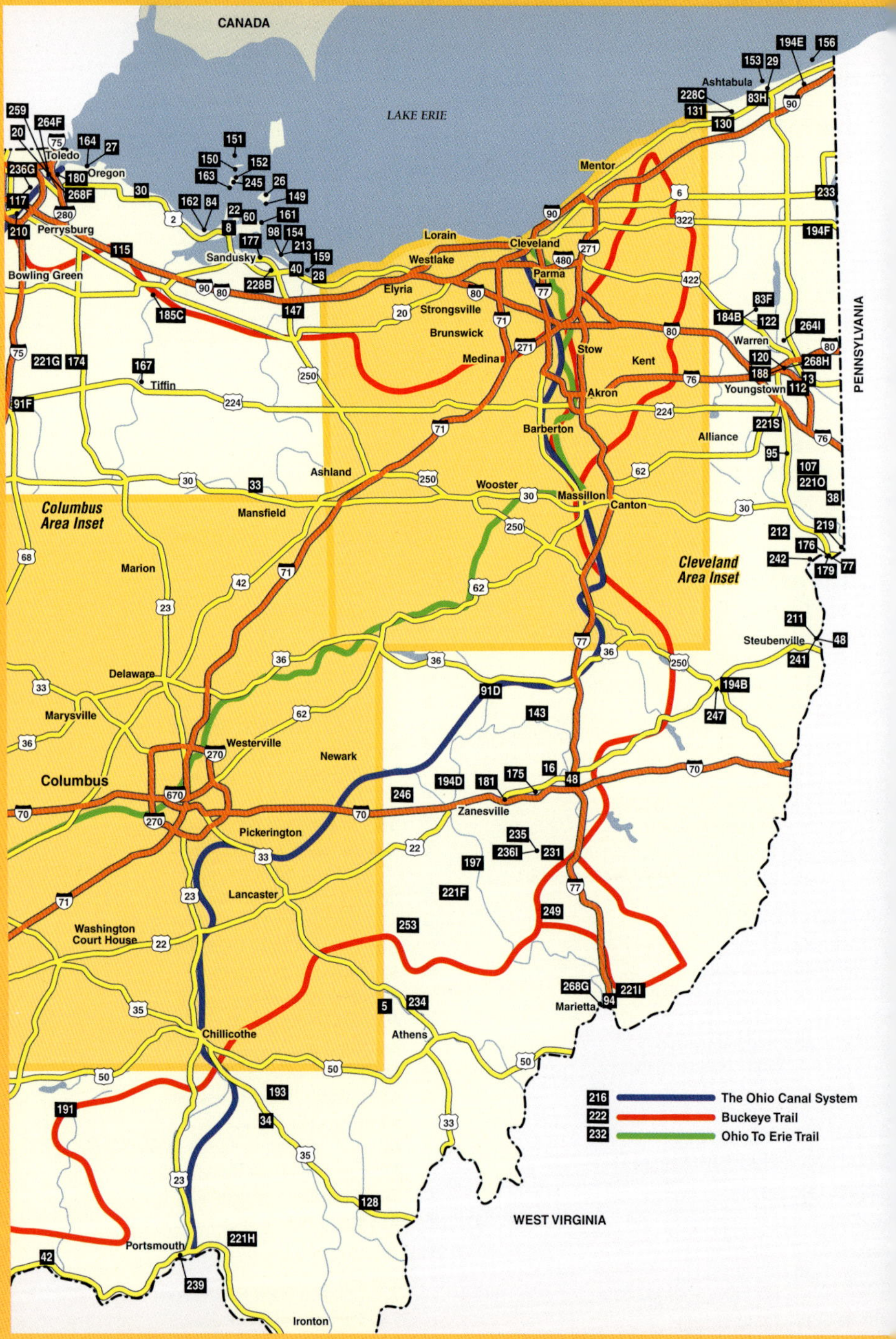

# CONTENTS

MAP 1 MAP 2 MAP 3 MAP 4 MAP 5

# MAP 3

## CINCINNATI AREA

# CONTENTS

MAP 1 MAP 2 MAP 3 MAP 4 MAP 5

# MAP 4

## COLUMBUS AREA

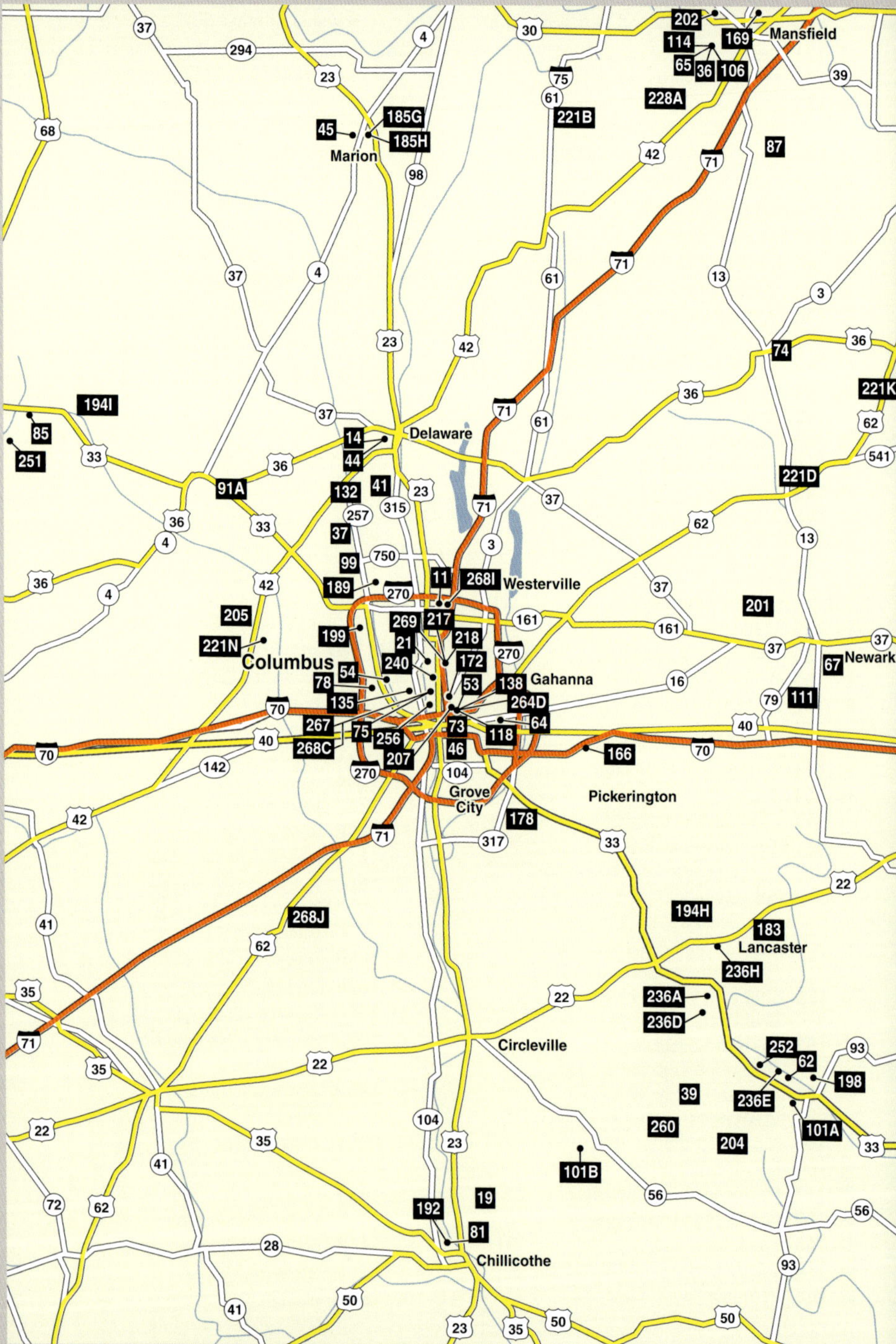

# CONTENTS

MAP 1 MAP 2 MAP 3 MAP 4 MAP 5

# MAP 5

## CLEVELAND AREA

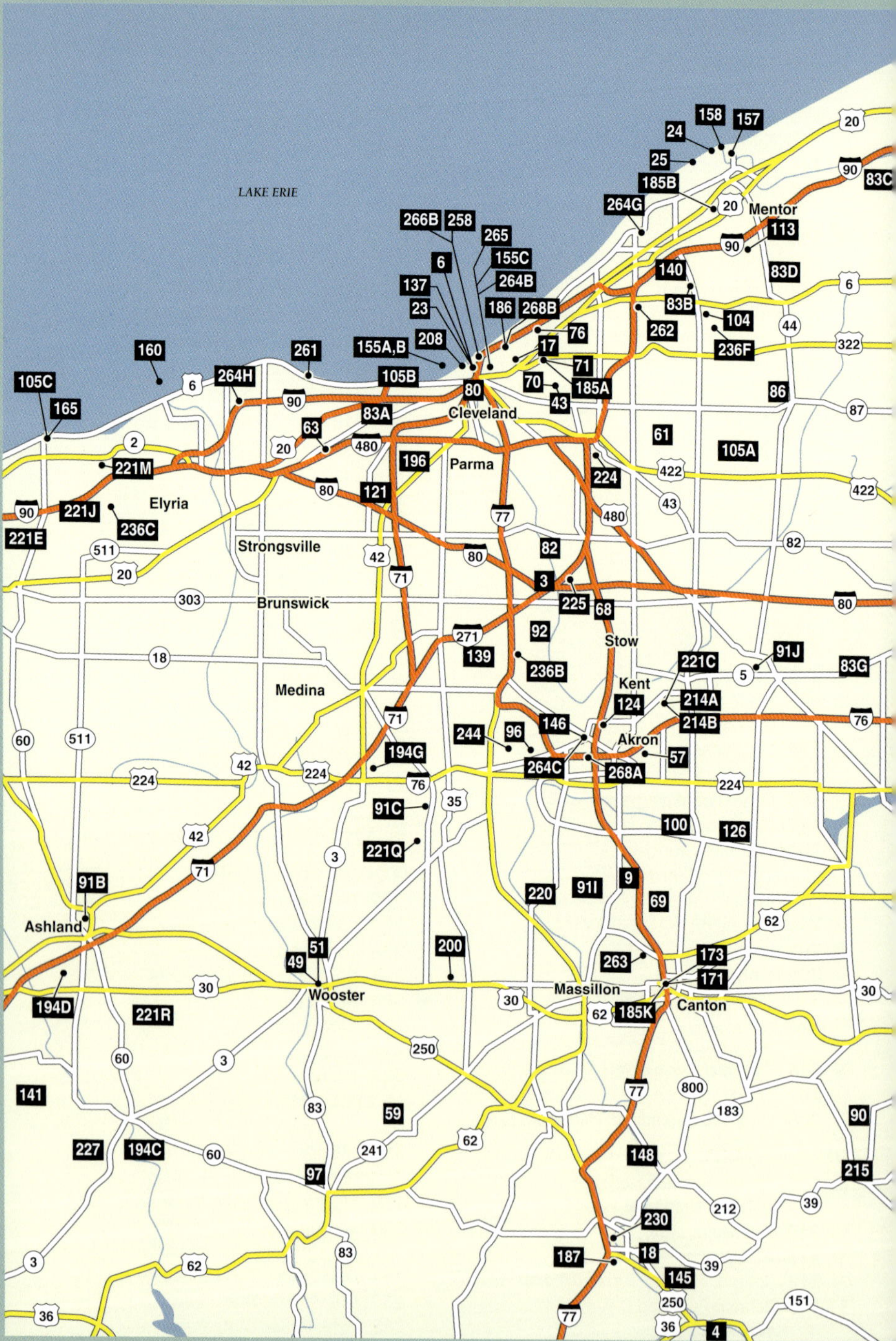

# CONTENTS

MAP 1 MAP 2 MAP 3 MAP 4 MAP 5

MUSKINGUM WATERSHED CONSERVANCY DISTRICT

ZIPLINE AND CANOPY TOURS

MOTORCYCLING

## INTRODUCTION

Welcome to Ohio, the Heart of it All!

Our state motto highlights not only our location in America's heartland but also our status as the center of many things. As you'll read here, Ohio is at the heart of aviation and space history, Underground Railroad history, rock and roll history, motorcycling history, and canal history.

We're also a state of firsts, from big things like the first professional baseball team (Cincinnati Red Stockings, 1869) to small things like oatmeal (Akron, 1877).

ROCK HOUSE/
HOCKING HILLS STATE PARK

Our inventors include, of course, Thomas Edison and the Wright brothers, but there are also African American Garrett Morgan, who invented both the gas mask (1914) and the traffic light (1923), and John William Lambert, who invented the first practical American gas-powered automobile in 1891.

The beauty of Ohio can be seen in the central flatlands, filled with miles of verdant farm fields, and in the south and east of the state, where twisting roads navigate the hills and valleys. The northern shorelines and islands dot Lake Erie from Ashtabula to Toledo.

Water recreation here can be as riotous as a water park on the Fourth of July or as peaceful as a fly fisherman silhouetted against a Clear Fork River sunset. A few of the state's 134 nature preserves are highlighted here. Some are primitive, meant for backcountry explorers who seek out hidden waterfalls and wildflowers. Others have established trails, recreational lakes, picnic areas, and restrooms.

And there are museums to love, from the sprawling National Museum of the U.S. Air Force to the small Central Ohio Fire Museum. Some are edifying, some are fun, and some are just quirky—dedicated to neon signs, bicycles, woodcarving, buttons, dolls, coal, and carousels.

Whichever way you choose to experience Ohio, you'll be happy you came.

ORVILLE WRIGHT IN FLIGHT, HUFFMAN PRAIRIE, DAYTON

## In Ohio, of course, there's plenty of airplane history to explore.

There are museums and history centers all over the state. Some of them even offer rides in vintage aircraft. For railroad adventure, check out the schedules and special events at these centers of railroad history.

*Welcome to*

# AIRPLANES & RAILROADS

**Ohio is often called the "birthplace of aviation" because the first aircraft was invented here.**

Ford Trimotor, a B-17, or even a P-51C "Red Tail" Tuskegee Airmen Mustang? You can do things like that here.

### 9 MAPS AIR MUSEUM ................7

**North Canton**

The Military Aircraft Preservation Society operates this museum at Akron-Canton Airport, dedicated to restoration, maintenance, and demonstration of historic military aircraft.

### 10 NATIONAL MUSEUM OF THE U.S. AIR FORCE ................8

**Dayton**

You can visit four presidential airplanes used by 11 different presidents. Be sure to stop at the top of the steps to offer a presidential wave to people below.

### 11 OHIO RAILWAY MUSEUM ................8

**Worthington**

Ride the *Red Bird,* the last CD&M interurban parlor car, as well as a Pullman passenger car and a vintage streetcar, all on one ticket at this museum.

*Find out more about*

# AIRPLANES & RAILROADS

## 1 ARMSTRONG AIR & SPACE MUSEUM

**500 Apollo Drive,**
**Wapakoneta, OH 45895**
**419-738-8811 or 800-860-0142**
**armstrongmuseum.org**

Walking up to this small museum in Wapakoneta inspires awe in any visitor. A 56-foot white sphere rises out of the green banks topped by angular concrete wings, suggesting a journey to the moon. The entrance is even more striking at night, when blue runway lights illuminate the sidewalk and the sphere glows. Neil Armstrong, and other Ohioans who have taken to the air, are honored here. The museum opened in 1972 in Armstrong's hometown. Exhibits include the first plane that 15-year-old Armstrong flew, an Aeronca Champion, as well as *Gemini* and *Apollo* memorabilia, interactive exhibits, and simulators. The lunar module simulator is especially exciting because you can feel pressure, manipulate controls, and imagine yourself in charge of a moon landing. The Astro Theater inside the dome offers views of the night sky and a 25-minute film of the *Apollo 11* moon landing.

## 2 CARILLON HISTORICAL PARK

**1000 Carillon Boulevard,**
**Dayton, OH 45409; 937-293-2841**
**cprss.org**
**advkeen.co/carillon**

You could spend days wandering through this 65-acre park and still not see everything. Focusing on transportation, though, is a good place to start, so begin at the Wright Brothers Aviation Center. Here you can see the 1905 *Wright Flyer III,* the first practical airplane, which is a National Historic Landmark. Moving along through the park, you can visit a replica of the Deeds barn, where inventor Charles Kettering and colleagues created the first electric self-starter for automobiles; the Carillon Park Rail and Steam Society's rideable 7.5-gauge miniature train; a full-size excursion train; a furnished 1894 train station originally located in Bowling Green; a 1907 railroad watchtower from Dayton; a collection of antique bicycles; the original Miami and Erie Canal Lock #17; and the James F. Dicke Family Transportation Center, which houses various railcars, cabooses, and trolley cars. (See also Dayton Aviation Heritage National Historic Park, page 133).

## 3 CUYAHOGA VALLEY SCENIC RAILROAD

**Peninsula Depot, 2325 Stine Road,**
**Peninsula, OH 44264**
**800-468-4070**
**cvsr.com**

There's something about a steam train engine that just gets people excited. First, you hear a clanking, hissing noise as the locomotive appears. It's so massive that it dwarfs the station and the crowd.

Steam billows out from beneath, and the wheels squall as the train slows to a stop. All aboard! Even if you only ride from one end of the Cuyahoga Valley to the other and back again, a trip aboard the Cuyahoga Valley Scenic Railroad is something to remember. Bicyclists and hikers are at every stop with another agenda, though. They hop on and off at stations along the way, get some exercise, then hop back on to return to their vehicles. Passengers can choose from coach, premium coach, first-class, or dome seating. A lounge car and an ADA car are also included. The café car offers snacks, soft drinks, beer, and wine. The CVSR hosts two-hour excursions for sightseeing, dining and drinks, entertainment, and children's activities. (See also Cuyahoga National Park page 146).

## 4 DENNISON RAILROAD DEPOT MUSEUM

**400 Center Street,**
**Dennison, OH 44621; 740-922-6776**
**dennisondepot.org**

Built in 1873, this National Historic Landmark is famous for its ties to World War II. Doing what they could to support the war effort, volunteers met service members at railroad stations all around the country, offering food, coffee, and moral support at free canteens. The 1.3 million people entertained here nicknamed this depot Dreamville, USA. The museum includes railroad exhibits, a gift shop, and a restaurant. On display are two steam locomotives, freight and passenger cars, and a military hospital car. A restored Pullman Sleeper is available as a bed-and-breakfast car. There is a Bing Scavenger Hunt for kids, an interactive railroad car, and a model train room. Oh, and coffee is still free for veterans at Lucille's Lunch Stand, named for a founder of the wartime canteen.

## 5 HOCKING VALLEY SCENIC RAILWAY

**33 West Canal Street,**
**Nelsonville, OH 45764; 740-753-9531**
**hvsry.org**

Operating on weekends and holidays, the railway offers countryside tours. Three diesel locomotives, as well as one steam locomotive, haul vintage passenger cars on easygoing scenic tours that include historic sights like Hocking Canal Lock #19 and the historic buildings of Haydenville, a company town for a brick-and-clay business. Others are holiday events like the popular Easter Bunny train (with an egg hunt) and the New Year's Eve special, which includes either pop and pizza or wine and cheese and finishes off with fireworks. Every summer, several train "robberies" are staged. In October, extra trains travel on Fridays to take advantage of fall foliage.

## 6 INTERNATIONAL WOMEN'S AIR & SPACE MUSEUM

**Burke Lakefront Airport,**
**1501 North Marginal Road, Suite 165,**
**Cleveland, OH 44114; 216-623-1111**
**iwasm.org/wp-blog**

Women have been part of air and space exploration since 1804, when Napoleon Bonaparte named Madame Blanchard, a famous balloonist, as chief air minister of ballooning. In the early 1900s, Katharine Wright assisted her famous brothers in making powered flight a practical reality. In World War II, Women's Air Force Service Pilots (WASPs) tested aircraft, flew transports, and towed targets. In 1961, 13 women were chosen as the first female astronaut trainees. These and other pioneers are remembered at this small, free museum. The IWASM also offers programs and lunch-and-learns. For schools and libraries, traveling exhibits are available.

## 7 LEBANON MASON MONROE RAILROAD

**16 East South Street,**
**Lebanon, OH 45036; 513-933-8022**
**lebanonrr.com**

On most weekends of the year, and some weekdays, you can board the Turtle Creek Valley Flyer here for a scenic country ride or a special event. For children's excursions, the railroad offers a Superhero TRAINing Adventure. Kids ride the train to a "top secret" location, where they can practice superhero moves and choose a "weapon" made by a balloon artist. Characters like Thomas the Train, Whyatt, Daniel Tiger, and Curious George travel on such children's excursions. There's also a Princess Express, which has a Magical Makeover that includes pixie dust. Adult train lovers can choose between scenic excursions, food- or holiday-themed rides, or a Murder Mystery Train. The Munich Express, with German-style food and drink, operates during the Lebanon Oktoberfest.

## 8 LIBERTY AVIATION MUSEUM

**Erie-Ottawa County International Airport, 3515 East State Road,**
**Port Clinton, OH 43452; 419-732-0234**
**libertyaviationmuseum.org**

This is a busy place, with more going on than aircraft displays. The museum's vintage planes come and go periodically to air shows and special events. Restoration is a key part of the museum's work, and visitors are welcome to observe. *Georgie's Gal,* a B-25J Mitchell Bomber from World War II, was restored there in 2011–12. A 1929 Ford Trimotor, which flew the Lake Erie island route for 50 years, was being restored in 2024. They've also acquired the *PT-728 Thomcat,* a World War II–era Vosper PT boat, which is currently undergoing restoration. Besides planes and the patrol torpedo boat, there's an eclectic collection of antique cars, motorcycles, and military vehicles. For instance, they have a 1947 Flxible Bus, the only known survivor of three buses built in Loudonville, Ohio, as mobile mooring masts for blimps. One of the very cool things at this museum is the Tin Goose Diner, a gorgeous 1950s-style restaurant. You might have to wait for seating, but the food and ambience are great. Junior Pilot Camps, car shows, book signings, and fly-ins by other vintage aircraft and helicopters sometimes include ride experiences.

## 9 MAPS AIR MUSEUM

**2260 International Parkway,**
**North Canton, OH 44720**
**330-896-6332**
**mapsairmuseum.org**

Even people like me who don't know much about military aircraft have heard the name Sopwith, the triplane famously flown by Snoopy in his dogfights with the Red Baron. A Sopwith Triplane replica, complete with a rotary engine and wooden propeller, is on display at MAPS. MAPS stands for Military Aviation Preservation Society, which makes this a working museum. Numerous vintage planes, plus helicopters, a glider, and a blimp, have been restored or are maintained here by volunteers. The museum is also home to original fighters and bombers like a Grumman F-14B Tomcat, a McDonnell F-101F Voodoo, and a Republic F-105 Thunderchief. The museum houses observation and training aircraft, military vehicles, flight simulators, and ordnance. Youth activities include a Civil Air Patrol squadron; Scout programs; and Air Academy, an introduction to flying for children 10 and older. Regular events like Scout days, fundraisers, car shows, and collector conventions are also on the museum schedule.

## 10 NATIONAL MUSEUM OF THE U.S. AIR FORCE

**1100 Spaatz Street, Wright-Patterson Air Force Base, Dayton, OH 45431**
**937-255-3286**
**nationalmuseum.af.mil**

Free admission and parking are great reasons to visit the vast museum at Wright-Patterson Air Force Base, but the best reason is to see the extensive collections of military flight history. Planes at the museum range from Eisenhower's *Air Force One* to a Lockheed AC-130A Spectre. Permanent exhibits cover the Wright Brothers, Civil War ballooning, the Doolittle Raiders, and the Tuskegee Airmen. In the Early Years Gallery, you can learn the story of the 1st Aero Squadron. It placed the first tactical air unit in the field when it joined Black Jack Pershing in Texas in 1916, in order to make reconnaissance flights into Mexico in the search for Pancho Villa. Besides maintaining extensive indoor and outdoor exhibits, the museum has active restoration and research divisions and offers programs for adults, teachers, students, and groups. Acres of parkland are dedicated to Memorial Park, where Air Force-associated units have placed more than 500 memorials to honor individuals, units, and organizations.

## 11 OHIO RAILWAY MUSEUM

**990 Proprietors Road, Worthington, OH 43085**
**614-885-7345**
**ohiorailwaymuseum.org**

Open only on Sunday afternoons May through December, this museum nevertheless offers a lot of value for day-trippers. Because it owns 2 miles of railroad right-of-way, the museum is able to offer visitors multiple rides on cars in their collection. On the railbed of the Columbus, Delaware, and Marion railway in Worthington, this museum collects locomotives, rail cars, streetcars, and interurban cars. One of their showpieces is the last CD&M interurban parlor car, the *Red Bird*. Their locomotive collection includes steam, electric, and diesel equipment. At the depot, collections of railroading culture and technology are on display.

CUYAHOGA VALLEY SCENIC RAILROAD, PENINSULA

CINCINNATI MUSIC HALL FRONTED BY DANCING LIGHTS IN THE CITY PARK

**Outdoor drama, ballet, symphonies, fine art, and Broadway musicals—Ohio has it all.**

Cleveland is home to one of the largest theater districts outside New York City. Ohio also boasts three outdoor dramas and numerous fine art museums. Enjoy a symphony under the stars or a ballet at venues all around the state. Whether you prefer the Renaissance masters or the most cutting-edge mixed-media artists, you can find their work in Ohio.

# Welcome to THE ARTS

**12 ARONOFF CENTER FOR THE ARTS** ........ 13

**Cincinnati**

The Cincinnati Arts Association provides a home here for ballet, theater, music, and art.

**13 BUTLER INSTITUTE OF AMERICAN ART** ........ 13

**Youngstown**

The Butler's 20,000-piece collection includes not only old masters but also new ones.

**14 CENTRAL OHIO SYMPHONY** ........ 13

**Delaware**

This volunteer group turned professional ensemble can draw more than 8,000 for a holiday concert.

**15 CINCINNATI ART MUSEUM** ........ 14

**Cincinnati**

Proud to be the first purpose-built museum west of the Allegheny Mountains, its Native American and folk-art collections are highlights.

**16 THE LIVING WORD OUTDOOR DRAMA** ........ 14

**Cambridge**

A long-running Passion Play is presented here from mid-June through September. More than a hundred locals volunteer to spend their summers onstage and behind the scenes, year after year.

**17 PLAYHOUSE SQUARE** ........ 15

**Cleveland**

It's been called the world's biggest theater restoration project, and big is exactly the right word. Boasting nine separate theaters, Playhouse Square is proud to be one of the largest American performing arts centers outside of Broadway itself.

**18 SCHOENBRUNN AMPHITHEATRE** ........ 15

**New Philadelphia**

Home of *Trumpet in the Land,* the story of Ohio's first Christian community, this outdoor amphitheater also offers contemporary plays.

**19 SUGARLOAF MOUNTAIN AMPHITHEATRE** ........ 15

**Chillicothe**

Fights, falls, gunfire, and thundering horses erupt nightly for audiences at this outdoor drama theater, featuring *Tecumseh!,* the story of the Shawnee Indian leader of a multitribal confederacy.

**20 TOLEDO MUSEUM OF ART** ........ 16

**Toledo**

The sprawling 36-acre campus of TMA is a far cry from the two rooms its founders first rented for exhibition space in 1901. Take a class, tour the galleries, sit in on a lecture, or attend a concert.

**Powers Auditorium in Youngstown was built in 1931 as the original Warner Brothers Theatre.**

CEILING OF POWERS AUDITORIUM, YOUNGSTOWN

## *Find out more about*
## THE ARTS

### 12 ARONOFF CENTER FOR THE ARTS

**650 Walnut Street, Cincinnati, OH 45202**
**513-621-ARTS (2787)**
**cincinnatiarts.org/aronoff-center**

To spend a day or an evening immersed in the arts, Cincinnatians head downtown to Aronoff Music Hall. Broadway plays, musical theater, opera, ballet and dance troupes, and orchestras are at home here, providing a full and diverse schedule of events. The Weston Art Gallery boasts exhibition spaces featuring art in all media. Education is part of Aronoff's mission, and the center runs an "Artists on Tour" program and holds events and performances for schools.

### 13 BUTLER INSTITUTE OF AMERICAN ART

**524 Wick Avenue, Youngstown, OH 44502**
**330-743-1107**
**butlerart.com**

The Art in the Early Morning program makes exhibits at the Butler come alive for babies in strollers (and their parents), preschoolers (and their parents), and senior citizens. The free Thursday programs allow in-depth gallery visits with a docent and include an art activity for older children. Since 1919, the Butler has collected and preserved American art of all types. The permanent collection includes art from the 18th through 20th centuries, plus Western, contemporary, sports, and new media art, Americana and folk art, and African American art. Beecher Court at the museum hosts dinners, lectures, and concerts. Admission is free.

### 14 CENTRAL OHIO SYMPHONY

**24 East Winter Street, Delaware, OH 43015 (performance venue);**
**20 West Central Ave., Delaware, OH 43015 (office);**
**740-362-1799**
**centralohiosymphony.org**

From their home at Ohio Wesleyan University's Gray Chapel, the symphony's professional musicians have been serving central Ohio for 45 years with the motto "Engage the Community through Music." Besides maintaining a regular concert schedule at several venues, the group hosts various outreach programs that have included therapeutic drumming and the Library Card Program, which gives students free admission to events, as well as discounted rates for their parents. The symphony is currently directed by Maestro Jaime Morales-Matos. The symphony is sponsored by several local organizations, plus the Ohio Arts Council, Ohio Wesleyan University, and the National Endowment for the Arts. Check the symphony's website for performance dates and locations.

PLAYHOUSE SQUARE, CLEVELAND

## 15 CINCINNATI ART MUSEUM

**953 Eden Park Drive,**
**Cincinnati, OH 45202**
**513-721-2787 or 877-472-4226**
**cincinnatiartmuseum.org**

Back in 1876, the ladies of Cincinnati organized an association dedicated to bringing culture to the hinterlands. Ten years later, they opened the Cincinnati Art Museum, billed as "The Art Palace of the West." Today, that modest effort has come, through art, to involve full-scale community engagement. Parking is free, and tours offered every day except Monday give visitors an up-close-and-personal look at selected highlights of the museum collections. Monthly themed events welcome visitors after dark, and daytime programs include summer art camps, tours for young children, puppet shows, and more. A speakers' bureau travels through the community with programs for adult and family audiences. For digitally inclined art lovers, the museum's bimonthly podcasts cover not only art but food, sports, and popular culture.

## 16 THE LIVING WORD OUTDOOR DRAMA

**6010 College Hill Road,**
**Cambridge, OH 43725**
**740-439-2761**
**livingworddrama.org**

For 50 years, the story of Jesus Christ has unfolded onstage in Ohio's only outdoor Passion Play. With shows on Friday and Saturday nights through the summer months, there are also themed events like Scout Night, Biker Night, Canned Food Drive Night, 4-H Night, and Tour Bus Night, all of which fill the seats of the 400-seat amphitheater. The authentic and colorful sets designed by biblical dramatist Frank Roughton Harvey include the Temple, Herod's Palace, the Sanhedrin, the Via Dolorosa, Golgotha, and Christ's Tomb. All come to life as the story unfolds. Behind-the-Scenes and Front-Set tours precede every show. A youth and family rally is part of the summer schedule, and it features a children's day of games, crafts and lessons, interactions with animals, and food options.

## 17 PLAYHOUSE SQUARE

**1501 Euclid Avenue, Suite 200, Cleveland, OH 44115; 216-771-4444**
**playhousesquare.org**
**cleveland.com/onstage/index.ssf/2012/12/playhousesquare-area_spots_for.html**

For millions of Midwesterners, Playhouse Square is within easy reach for a day trip or an overnight excursion. Choose from nine theaters, including an outdoor performance space and restored historic theaters that date back to the Roaring Twenties. Patrons can choose from Broadway shows, music and dance, and children's performances. The Playhouse Square parking garage and Keybank State Theatre Lobby provide easy indoor access to the theaters. Resident companies that call Playhouse Square home include The City Club of Cleveland, Cleveland Ballet, Cleveland International Film Festival, Cleveland Play House, Cleveland State University Department of Theatre and Dance, DANCECleveland, Great Lakes Theater, and Tri-C JazzFest. For students, tours, bus subsidies, and private tours can be arranged. Packages that include tickets, lodging, and parking are available. Before or after your show, pick out a restaurant or bistro from the dozens in the theater district.

## 18 SCHOENBRUNN AMPHITHEATRE

**1600 Trumpet Drive Northeast, New Philadelphia, OH 44663**
**330-339-1132**
**trumpetintheland.com**

The first time I saw the outdoor drama *Trumpet in the Land*, I was still young enough to be open-mouthed and wide-eyed. Horses galloped across the stage, Native Americans danced, rifles cracked, and tension mounted until the bone-chilling finale. Instantly, I became a lifelong fan of live theater. *Trumpet,* the premier attraction of Schoenbrunn Amphitheatre, tells the story of Moravian missionary David Zeisberger, his pioneer settlement, and the infamous Gnadenhutten Massacre, in which 96 Moravian Christian Lenape Indians were killed by Colonial militiamen, five years before the Revolutionary War. A revolving cast of actors, many of whom participate for years, is drawn mostly from the surrounding community. The amphitheater also hosts contemporary plays throughout the summer season, as well as holiday-themed events. Bring a rain poncho, just in case, and prepare to be thrilled and chilled by the emotional and passionate story of the Ohio frontier.

## 19 SUGARLOAF MOUNTAIN AMPHITHEATRE

**5968 Marietta Road, Chillicothe, OH 45601; 866-775-0700**
**tecumsehdrama.com**

The spectacular outdoor drama *Tecumseh!* has enthralled audiences here since 1973. Live cannon fire erupts onstage, horses barrel through the water, torches ignite, and loincloths flutter as the story unfolds under the stars on summer nights. Tecumseh was a Shawnee Indian who led a large confederacy of

Native Americans who wanted to keep settlers out of the Ohio country. With his brother Tenskwatawa, who was renowned as the Prophet, he fought from present-day Chillicothe to the wilds of what is now Ontario. The brothers were involved in the Battle of Tippecanoe and in the War of 1812, when a Native American confederacy allied with the British. Tecumseh's death during the Battle of the Thames in Canada ended the confederacy, which withered away thereafter.

Besides the drama, the 1,800-seat amphitheater hosts a military appreciation night, and an October Frankenstein Experience that includes vintage horror movie showings, an escape room, and a haunted trail.

## 20 TOLEDO MUSEUM OF ART

**2445 Monroe Street, Toledo, OH 43620; 800-644-6862**
**toledomuseum.org**

Walking through the glittering displays of the Glass Pavilion, you might find yourself wanting to try your hand at glass art. Could you do it? It's easy to find out at one of TMA's Glass Art Workshops. From a flashy firework paperweight to a delicate, multicolored fish, participants can unleash their inner artist and take home a one-of-a-kind, very personal keepsake. Workshops in glass are among many offered to children, teens, and adults at TMA. All the classes are linked to museum exhibits and include gallery tours. Scholarships are offered for the workshops. A poetry contest includes both youth and adults, and entries must be inspired by art. Adult poetry workshops are also available. The TMA campus includes not only the Glass Pavilion but also five other buildings that house an exhibition space with 30,000 works of art, a concert hall, a lecture hall, classrooms, and more. El Greco, Cézanne, Rembrandt, and Picasso are among the artists represented. Admission is free except for special exhibitions.

## 21 WEXNER CENTER FOR THE ARTS

**1871 North High Street, Columbus, OH 43210; 614-292-3535**

Adventurous art lovers will find plenty to love at the Wex, especially since gallery admissions and tours are free of charge. Contemporary artists working in a variety of media are showcased in the galleries of the Wexner Center at The Ohio State University. Classic, foreign, and independent films are always on tap, and music, theater, dance, and lectures rotate on the Wexner stages. Artists' residencies are awarded in all disciplines. For the public, classes from filmmakers, curators, and choreographers are all available. You can attend book signings and free guided exhibition tours. Senior showcases and ASL tours are also available. For youth, there are video competitions, boot camps, social events, and a yearly family film festival.

CENTRAL OHIO SYMPHONY, DELAWARE

HEADLANDS DUNES STATE NATURE PRESERVE, MENTOR

## Ohio doesn't seem like a beach state, but it is.

Toes in the sand, Ohioans enjoy miles of beaches along Lake Erie. We don't have much in the way of seashells, but searching for beach glass is a favorite hobby here. Glass that's clear, green, cobalt blue, seafoam, and light purple is lying around, waiting to be found. There's even a Beach Glass Festival in Ashtabula.

# Welcome to BEACHES & DUNES

*Find out more about*

# BEACHES & DUNES

## 22 EAST HARBOR STATE PARK

**1169 North Buck Road, Lakeside-Marblehead, OH 43440**
**419-734-4424**
**ohiodnr.gov/go-and-do/plan-a-visit/find-a-property/east-harbor-state-park**

If you close your eyes and use your senses, you might have trouble believing you're in the Midwest. Gentle waves lap at the sand, seagulls caw, a nice breeze ruffles your hair, and sunshine pours down. Sand crunches between your toes. Children shriek and giggle, parents call out, and you can smell barbecue from the picnic ground next door. Open your eyes to see a 1,500-foot beach sprawling across the Lake Erie shoreline. Early in the mornings, walkers and joggers measure out their exercise. Families crowd the beach on sunny days, and even cloudy ones. Late at night, people are still stargazing and enjoying the lakeside ambience. The well-maintained bathrooms and changing rooms also include outdoor showers.

EAST HARBOR STATE PARK, LAKESIDE-MARBLEHEAD

## 23 EDGEWATER PARK

**6500 Cleveland Memorial Shoreway, Cleveland, OH 44144; 216-635-3200**
**advkeen.co/edgewater**

Part of the impressive Cleveland Metroparks system, Edgewater Beach boasts a new $3 million Beach House restaurant, where friends gather for a meal and drinks on the second-level deck. Down on the 2,400-foot beach, amenities include a dog-friendly area, a volleyball court, shelters, a fishing pier, and a 1,000-foot swimming area. For the fitness-minded, kayaks, paddleboards, and walking paths are available. Yoga classes start at 7 a.m. Clevelanders gather up their blankets and beach chairs on summer Thursday nights for Edgewater LIVE, a concert series with local bands. Music lovers can also take advantage of rotating local food trucks, craft beer, and beach-themed cocktails.

## 24 FAIRPORT HARBOR LAKEFRONT BEACH

**301 Huntington Beach Drive, Fairport Harbor, OH 44077**
**440-639-9972**
**advkeen.co/fairport**

Even your dog has a place to swim at this small beach near Fairport Lighthouse. The pet area is off to one side and allows Fido and friends to enjoy the water. The main beach has a parking area (it has a small fee) and also offers concessions, restrooms, and showers. A wheelchair-accessible boardwalk is senior-friendly and lined with benches and picnic tables. Fairport Beach is also a great place to learn a water sport. There's an extensive summer schedule of private 90-minute lessons on kayaks, paddleboards, sailboats, and personal watercraft. Equipment is available, or you can bring your own. Group lessons, known as Outreach Adventures, provide an hour of instruction and all equipment for groups of 10–30.

## 25 HEADLANDS DUNES STATE NATURE PRESERVE

**9601 Headlands Road, Mentor, OH 44060; 614-265-6561**
**advkeen.co/headlands**

If you want to see an Ohio beach the way the Native Americans did, come here, to one of the only preserved natural beaches in the state. The preserve is adjacent to Headlands Beach State Park, outside Mentor, and also next to the Fairport Harbor West Breakwater Light, which is privately owned and not open to the public. You can, however, get pretty close to it along a breakwater trail. The microcosm of plants and animals here begins with switchgrass and beach grass, which catch and stabilize drifting sand. The area provides a sanctuary for migrating birds and monarch butterflies. Marked trails and a boardwalk provide safe access for visitors and protection for the fragile ecosystem.

## 26 KELLEYS ISLAND STATE PARK BEACH

**920 Division Street,**
**Kelleys Island, OH 43438**
**419-746-2546**
**advkeen.co/kelleysisland**

There's no lifeguard, but the water is shallow, so the beach at Kelleys Island is a good place for families to kick back and relax during their island visit. Even if you're not a swimmer, you can enjoy the water here because the sandy shelf extends 100 feet into the lake, and you can wade to your heart's content. The island's scenic Glacial Grooves are across the road, and the state park's fishing pier, boat ramp, and walking trails are nearby. There are restrooms and changing rooms, plus kayak rentals. A number of ferry services (including car ferries) are available to take you to the island.

GLACIAL GROOVES IN KELLEYS ISLAND STATE PARK, KELLEYS ISLAND

ROCKY SHORELINE AT MAUMEE BAY STATE PARK, OREGON

## 27 MAUMEE BAY STATE PARK BEACH

**1400 State Park Road, Oregon, OH 43616; 419-836-7758**
**advkeen.co/maumee**

Beachgoers have two choices here. You can opt for the half-mile lakeside beach, or move a short distance to a 57-acre inland lake, which also has a sandy beach, plus a lifeguard. Personal watercraft are available for rent on the Lake Erie side, as are canoes, kayaks, and paddleboats at the inland lake. An amphitheater between the beaches hosts weekend entertainment during the summer.

## 28 NICKEL PLATE BEACH

**Nickel Plate Drive, Huron, OH 44839**
**419-433-8487**
**advkeen.co/nickelplate**

Ohio's largest beach, just east of the Huron River, has soft natural sand, picnic areas, and restrooms. There's a $5 parking fee during the summer, but winter visits for beach walking and bicycling are free. Small, flat stones can be found on the beach and are popular for skipping and rock painting. The play areas include an outdoor Ping-Pong table and beach volleyball courts (bring your own equipment). Be sure to get a picture of the giant Adirondack chair. Visitors should remember that there is no lifeguard on duty, and potentially dangerous rip currents have been known to occur here.

## 29 WALNUT BEACH PARK

**Lake Avenue and Walnut Boulevard, Ashtabula, OH 44004**
**440-992-7103**
**advkeen.co/walnut_beach**

Long stretches of pretty, foot-friendly beach are here, making it a great place to search for beach glass—manmade glass that has been rounded by the waves. The 28-acre park has plenty of amenities, starting with the Ashtabula Harbor Light on one side, plus a 1.4-mile breakwater for fishing. There is a wheelchair-accessible boardwalk, a nature trail, and walkways over dunes and wetlands. Courts for beach volleyball and basketball are here, along with a skate park and playground. The Great Ohio Lake-to-River Greenway has its northern terminus at the park. An annual Beach Glass Festival is held at the harbor in June, attracting collectors and artists.

**Lake Erie is the 12th largest freshwater lake in the world, and 312 miles of its shoreline fall in Ohio.**

CAPE MAY WARBLER, MAGEE MARSH

**As free and wild as songbirds and raptors appear, they can be frighteningly dependent on us for their very existence.**

An owlet in a contaminated habitat, a hawk that's been struck by a car, or even a human-raised crow may never be able to survive unprotected. They remind us of our responsibility to nature and its inhabitants. Birds are protected statewide in nature preserves, where day-trippers may also catch glimpses of other wildlife. Some preserves are known for their geological features, others for their profusion of wildflowers. Still others protect original forests, wetlands, and prairies. Most feature hiking trails that allow visitors to enjoy nature without disturbing delicate ecosystems.

*Welcome to*

# BIRDS & NATURE

**Ohio enjoys astounding biodiversity. One stunning example is the Big Darby Creek, which is home to more freshwater mussels than Europe and Australia combined.**

*Find out more about*

# BIRDS & NATURE

## 30 BLACK SWAMP BIRD OBSERVATORY

**13551 West State Route 2, Oak Harbor, OH 43449; 419-898-4070**
**bsbo.org**

If you've ever thought you might like to dip a toe into the birding world, Black Swamp is the place to start. Your first excursion might be a walk along the modest ⅓-mile birding trail behind the visitor center. If you're intrigued by the migrant songbirds there, or the peculiar antics of the American woodcock, your next step is attending a Where the Birds Are popup trip, or the once-a-year field trip to see wintering raptors and waterfowl at Killdeer Plains. Research, education, and conservation are the missions of the Observatory, and enthusiastic birders and volunteers are always welcome.

## 31 CLIFTON GORGE STATE NATURE PRESERVE

**2381 State Route 343,**
**Yellow Springs, OH 45387**
**614-265-6453**
**advkeen.co/clifton_gorge**

You might imagine canyons are only found out West, but we've got them right here in southwest Ohio. Clifton Gorge, one of 136 State Nature Preserves in Ohio, is also one of 23 National Natural Landmarks in the state. Set amid 268 acres along the Little Miami River, the Gorge is a spectacular example of the ways in which glacial rivers cut through limestone and dolomite bedrock. In this case, geologists speculate that glacial "potholes" (lakes left behind by melting glacier ice) may have connected to form one especially deep-and-narrow channel. Sections of rapids and waterfalls are visible from the trail along the Little Miami River. The Gorge trail is especially known for spring displays of snow trillium.

## 32 CRABILL FEN STATE NATURE PRESERVE

**Buck Creek State Park,**
**1901 Buck Creek Lane,**
**Springfield, OH 45502**
**937-322-5284**
**GPS: 39.9622823°, -83.7513158°**
**trekohio.com/clark**

Crabill Fen, named for a pioneer family, is a spring-fed alkaline wetland at the edge of the Kennard glacial outwash in Buck Creek State Park. There are no visitor facilities or trails in the fen, but nature lovers will find it worthwhile for the unusual plant species preserved there. These include prairie dock, limestone savory, fen Indian plantain, fen sedge, and blue-leaved willow, among others. Ecological management, including removal and treatment of invasive species, keeps the fen protected. Because the fen is a sensitive area, access is by downloadable permit from the ODNR Division of Natural Areas and Preserves; request at least 14 days in advance.

## 33 CRAWFORD PARK DISTRICT

**2401 State Route 598, Crestline, OH 44827; 419-683-9000 crawfordparkdistrict.org**

Two parks, three nature preserves, a wildlife area, and a bikeway make up this park district serving Crawford County in northern Ohio. The 53-acre **Unger Park** has a 3-mile trail system that includes sections open to horses from June through October. Yearly prescribed burns keep the restored prairie healthy. Unger also features more than 100 species of reintroduced prairie plants and a pond and wetland habitat, offering hikers the same views early explorers and settlers would have seen. **Lowe-Volk Park Nature Center** near Crestline displays exhibits, including live wildlife. It features 2 miles of trails, a fishing dock, and a boardwalk. **Sears Woods State Nature Preserve** is known for abundant spring wildflowers, songbirds, and wood frogs. **Heckert Nature Preserve** is known for butterflies, some of which overwinter here. **The Daughmer Prairie Savannah** preserves a 74-acre remnant of Sandusky Plain, an unplowed, deep-soil land, with species including prairie cord grass, Bicknell's sedge, wheat sedge, and flat-stemmed spike-rush. At the **Sandusky Wildlife Area,** a yearly drawing allows a limited number of hunters from Crawford County. The **Barb Dolch Memorial Bikeway,** formerly the Colonel Crawford Bikeway, boasts 32 miles that wind through several of the parks and preserves. One stop is at a monument that honors Col. Crawford, captured and killed by Native Americans in 1782. **Sandusky Headwaters Preserve** was opened in 2021 for pas-

SANDUSKY WILDLIFE AREA, CRAWFORD COUNTY

sive recreation. Its 38 acres at the headwaters of the Sandusky River include old-growth forests, in addition to manmade wetland ponds and vernal pools and a recreated wetland/marsh prairie.

## 34 LAKE KATHARINE STATE NATURE PRESERVE

**1703 Lake Katharine Road,**
**Jackson, OH 45640; 740-286-2487**
**GPS: 39.085907°, -82.669624°**
**advkeen.co/lake_katharine**

Lake Katharine is one of the little-known gems of southwest Ohio. Surrounded by a 2,019-acre preserve, the wildflower display here includes native orchids and both bigleaf and umbrella magnolias. The western side of the preserve is closed to visitors, but elsewhere, Calico Bush, Salt Creek, and Pine Ridge trails are available to hikers. The 5.5 miles of trails lead visitors across creeks, through marshlands, and under the edges of massive sandstone cliffs. The 120-acre artificial lake is open only to permit holders for a fee. Those seeking to use the lake can call the park office the last Friday of the month to request a permit. Boats must be carried in; boat motors are not allowed. Five per day are issued Fridays through Mondays between April and October, sunrise to sunset. Limited hunting is sometimes permitted in the preserve.

## 35 MUD LAKE BOG STATE NATURE PRESERVE

**Northwest Township, Williams County,**
**Edon, OH; 614-265-6453**
**GPS: 41.6481056°, -84.7680119°**
**advkeen.co/mudlake**

This unique kettle-hole lake is bordered by an alkaline fen on one side and an acidic sphagnum bog on the other. The combination must be good for insect life because many dragonfly and damselfly species thrive here, including the lily pad forktail, marsh bluet, Canada darner, and mottled darner. Some of the 26 plant species found at Mud Lake Bog are swamp birch, shrubby cinquefoil, and lesser bladderwort. Because the 74-acre bog is a sensitive area, access is by downloadable permit from the ODNR Division of Natural Areas and Preserves; request at least 14 days in advance.

## 36 OHIO BIRD SANCTUARY

**3774 Orweiler Road,**
**Mansfield, OH 44903; 419-884-4295**
**ohiobirdsanctuary.com**

If you get past the "ick" factor, get a cup of mealworms at the visitor center before you tour the sanctuary. The aviary residents will appreciate it. Besides songbirds in the aviary, raptors and vultures unable to survive in the wild are housed in outdoor cages. You might even see wild vultures visiting their injured kin. The 90-acre sanctuary is home to some 52 species of migratory and resident birds. Outdoor aviaries are wheelchair and stroller accessible. Four miles of hiking trails wind through the preserve, including a wheelchair-accessible boardwalk on the Wood Duck Trail. The sanctuary does educational outreach and offers field trips and nature camps for student groups. New in 2021 is the Treehouse Classroom, which immerses students in the treetops. The educational building is available for corporate retreats and meetings, parties and celebrations, and even weddings.

## 37 OHIO WILDLIFE CENTER

**6131 Cook Road, Powell, OH 43065**
**614-734-9453**
**ohiowildlifecenter.org**

At the Ohio Wildlife Center, amphibians, reptiles, small and large mammals, raptors, turkeys, waterfowl, and migratory birds find homes when they can no longer live in the wild. Outreach programs, day camps, Scout programs, and guided tours introduce visitors to the varied wildlife at the center. A regular lecture series is offered to the public and covers such topics as drinking water safety, bees, nocturnal animals, tree identification, and more. Historic Bonner Barn, originally built in 1891, provides space for 100 people to celebrate weddings and family events, hold meetings or retreats, or just throw a party. The center is not open daily, so be sure to check the schedule before visiting. It is generally open to the public on the second Sunday of the month, from noon to 2 p.m.

## 38 SHEEPSKIN HOLLOW STATE NATURE PRESERVE

**51766 Pancake-Clarkson Road, Negley, OH 44441; 614-265-6419**
**advkeen.co/sheepskin_hollow**

Spring is a great time to visit the Hollow, when red trillium, hepatica, and pink lady's slipper are blooming, but the flora and fauna are complex and fascinating any time of year. Eastern hemlocks and mesophytic plants fill the hollow. Lichens, algae, and fungi cling to sandstone and shale outcrops. A headwater stream is occupied by fish, salamanders, and frogs.

Part of the charm of Sheepskin Hollow Falls is the adventure you'll have getting there. First, you stroll along an abandoned railbed, then hike up a hill and down again into the hollow. After that, you'd better have waterproof boots to navigate up the stream to the falls. Because this is a remote area, there are no restrooms or organized trail systems.

## 39 SHEICK HOLLOW STATE NATURE PRESERVE

**Laurel Township, Hocking County**
**ohiodnr.gov/buy-and-apply/special-use-permits/nature-preserve-access**

Black Hand sandstone, known for forming sheer cliffs and gorges throughout Ohio, surrounds narrow, fern-filled Scheick Hollow, which is home to hemlock, birch, and Canada yew. Seasonal waterfalls provide a cool environment for rare nesting birds that attract bird-watchers. Green warblers found here include magnolia, Canada, and black-throated species. Hermit thrushes and solitary vireos can also be spotted. The hollow and its floodplain are also home to a number of slump blocks (accumulated material that has slid or fallen). Access is by downloadable permit from the ODNR Division of Natural Areas and Preserves; request at least 14 days in advance.

## 40 SHELDON MARSH STATE NATURE PRESERVE

**2715 Cleveland Road West, Huron, OH 44839; 614-265-6419**
**advkeen.co/sheldon_marsh**

Along Sandusky Bay, the rare coastal wetland habitat of Sheldon Marsh provides a home, or at least a safe stopover, for some 300 bird species. In the summertime, bird-watchers can spot great blue herons, red-tailed hawks, black-crowned night herons, wood ducks, common terns, woodcocks, and great horned owls, as well as many species of songbirds. In the spring, wildflowers spotted at the preserve include the spectacularly spiky cardinal flower, plus Dutchman's breeches and cut-leaved toothwort. Later blooms include trout lilies, trilliums, wild ginger, and wild geraniums. The parking lot and 2 miles of trails are wheelchair accessible. Hikers can access the beach from the trail system.

## 41 STRATFORD WOODS STATE NATURE PRESERVE

**3083 Liberty Road, Delaware, OH 43015; 740-363-2548**
**advkeen.co/stratford_woods**

Two buttonbush swamps occupy the north section of Stratford Woods. Also called shrub swamps, these transitional areas are freshwater wetland ecosystems that occupy a niche halfway between wetter "true" swamps and drier marshes. Pin oak and swamp white oak are present in Stratford's buttonbush swamps. The south section is drier and includes Delaware limestone bedrock in a ravine. A stream in this section is festooned every spring by mayapples, dwarf larkspur, and blue phlox, among other wildflowers. The 95-acre preserve is home to more than 30 species of trees, including oak, hickory, ash, and maple. Amenities at the preserve include a parking lot, 4 miles of loop trails, restrooms, and an outdoor education center.

## 42 WHIPPLE STATE NATURE PRESERVE

**1194 State Route 247, Manchester, OH 45144; 614-265-6419**
**advkeen.co/whipple**

Geology buffs appreciate Whipple (named for land donor Robert A. Whipple) for its examples of slump blocks (material that has accumulated after falling downhill), dolomite cliffs that can rise to 30 feet, and the mysterious springs and sinkholes along a narrow ridgetop. Flower lovers are thankful for the luxurious displays of spring wildflowers and ferns. The 448-acre preserve is available to nature lovers and hikers along 2 miles of moderately difficult loop trail. Park carefully because space for cars is limited in the pull-off area. There are no restrooms.

CLIFF OF BLACK HAND SANDSTONE OVERHANGING A SEASONAL WATERFALL THAT GRACES ASH CAVE, HOCKING HILLS

THE BOOK LOFT, GERMAN VILLAGE, COLUMBUS

## If you're a reader, then you know the feeling of walking into a charming bookstore.

You take a deep breath, break into a big smile, and maybe do a little twirl of happiness. Then you browse. Should you start with the new releases? Will it be the latest beach read, something from your favorite author, or a great nonfiction tome a friend recommended? Maybe you'd rather start at the back and work your way forward. The possibilities are endless. Independent bookstores, happily, often have a resident cat or dog to keep you company as you browse. These stores can keep you on the road for many, many miles of pleasurable day trips.

# *Welcome to* BOOKS, BOOKS & MORE BOOKS



**Cleveland Heights**

Appletree Books has been around since 1975. Staff members aren't just book fans but art lovers, too, so there's always something cool to see as you browse the reads.



**Delaware**

People of all ages will love Beanbag Books. There's plenty to keep kids engaged, plus regular chairs for adults who want to sit somewhere other than a beanbag.



**Marion**

Birch Tree Bookery is the only independent bookstore in Marion, embracing the power of books have to foster community. Stop in and support local booksellers.



**German Village, Columbus**

Bibliophiles from all over make the trip to Columbus just to visit the store with 32 rooms of books.



**Cincinnati**

The mission of Bookery Cincy is to provide readers with "books that scream to be finished." Stop by, and the staff will help you find the kind of book that will keep you up all night reading because you can't put it down.



**Steubenville**

This charming bookstore in downtown Steubenville draws you in with promises of quirky finds.



**Wooster**

If you're looking for used and rare books, this store can help. You can buy, sell, and trade books, selecting from more than 80,000 titles.



**Madeira**

Besides the latest best-selling novels, you'll find an interesting selection of historical fiction and nonfiction.



**Wooster**

For nearly 40 years, this annual event has drawn local and national authors and illustrators for a two-day fall festival of books.

**Superman was invented by two guys in Cleveland just before WWII, and many of their early stories featured Superman fighting Nazis.**

### 52 CINCY BOOK BUS DEPOT ........ 39

**Sharonville**

The Cincy Book Bus looks like something out of a storybook. This retro VW is not only cool, but it's also a clever way to draw people in. Customers can also meet owner Melanie Moore, who handpicks the books herself.

### 53 COLUMBUS BOOK FESTIVAL ........ 39

**Columbus**

National, local, and indie authors are celebrated in a free two-day festival at the city's main library and in Topiary Park.

### 54 COVER TO COVER: BOOKS FOR YOUNG READERS ........ 40

**Columbus**

Stop by this children's bookstore for a Saturday morning story time or to pick something from its great selection of literature for young readers. The store also hosts a variety of events with authors and illustrators.

### 55 DARK STAR BOOKS ........ 40

**Yellow Springs**

In this comfortably crowded used bookstore, you can find everything from vintage comics to science fiction to art and philosophy.

### 56 DOWNBOUND BOOKS ........ 40

**Cincinnati**

They don't have a lot of space in their Northside bookstore, so the folks at Downbound Books are careful to include an eclectic mix of reading material that they hope you'll enjoy.

**57 ELIZABETH'S BOOKSHOP & WRITING CENTRE** ................ 40

**Akron**

The mission at Elizabeth's is to recognize marginalized voices. To that end, they host book groups and meetups, local author meet-and-greets, and workshops.

**58 EPIC BOOK SHOP** .................. 40

**Yellow Springs**

The specialties here are books on religion, philosophy, literature, healing, and the occult. They also carry selections of incense and icons.

**59 FAITH VIEW BOOKS** ............ 40

**Fredericksburg**

Pick up your free cup of coffee and start browsing. At Faith View you'll find faith-based storybooks, Bibles, and a large children's section.

**60 THE FINE PRINT BOOKSHOP** ................ 41

**Lakeside Marblehead**

It's a full-service bookstore, but at Fine Print, kids rule.

**61 FIRESIDE BOOKSHOP** .......... 41

**Chagrin Falls**

Author events here have even featured a dog and a horse. Two long-time employees own the shop now, which first opened in 1963.

**62 FOX'S BOOK ADVENTURES** ............ 41

**Logan**

Is there anything better than ice cream or a good book? At Fox's Book Adventures, you can get both. If that doesn't convince you to visit, your kids will.

**63 GODDESS ELITE** ...................... 41

**North Olmstead**

As a New Age and metaphysical store, Goddess Elite carries books on tarot, spellcasting, oracles, divination, and animal magic.

**64 GRAMERCY BOOKS** ............. 42

**Bexley**

Gramercy Books takes its name from the French term *grand merci*, which means "big thanks" or "many thanks." The staff and owners of this independent bookstore are grateful for their vibrant book community.

**65 HOLLY'S BOOK RACK** .......... 42

**Ontario**

This spacious, well-organized bookstore carries new and used books, as well as audiobooks.

**66 JOSEPH-BETH BOOKSELLERS** ....................... 42

**Cincinnati**

Serving as a host for authors, celebrities, politicians, and public figures is a large part of Joseph-Beth's mission.

**67 KICKS MIX BOOKSTORE** .................. 42

**Newark**

At Kicks Mix Bookstore, you can find new and used books and other media. It's an eclectic independent shop; and while browsing, you just might see one of the owner's cats.

**68 THE LEARNED OWL BOOK SHOP** ............................ 42

**Hudson**

It's groovy! That's what their mascot, an owl, says about this three-story book shop. Possibly the grooviest thing is that they not only host programs with local authors but also with children's book characters.

### 69 LITTLE SPARROW BOOKSHOP ....... 42

**North Canton**

This cozy independent bookshop is proud to offer the warm experience you can only get in community bookshops. It also works hard to support local authors.

### 70 LOGANBERRY BOOKS ......... 43

**Shaker Heights**

With more than 100,000 new and used books to choose from, you can't go wrong at Loganberry's. The stars of its collection are children's books, women's literature and history, and fine and performing arts.

### 71 MAC'S BACKS-BOOKS ON COVENTRY........ 43

**Cleveland Heights**

Three book clubs meet here regularly. One focuses on literary fiction and nonfiction, one on science fiction, and one on LGBTQ+ topics.

### 72 NEW AND OLD PAGES BOOK SHOPPE ........................ 44

**Englewood**

This used bookstore is a great place to go if you're looking for a bargain. It carries new and used books for purchase, but customers can bring books for trade. The store also frequently hosts events.

### 73 OHIOANA BOOK FESTIVAL..................... 44

**Columbus**

If you're a book lover, a book reader, a bookseller, or a book writer, this is the quintessential festival for you. Ohioana hosts a full day of networking, browsing, and bookselling.

### 74 PARAGRAPHS BOOKSTORE ............................ 44

**Mt. Vernon**

The staff at Paragraphs loves to put the right book in the hands of the right person. They also love browsers and provide comfortable chairs in which patrons can try out new books.

### 75 PROLOGUE BOOKSHOP.............................. 44

**Columbus**

The power of reading and literature is important at this bookstore, which is vocal about the benefits of shopping locally. Besides five book clubs, Prologue also offers a silent book club meant especially for introverts.

### 76 THE READING ROOM ........... 44

**Cleveland**

The Reading Room is an activist-run nonprofit that aims to promote social equality through literacy. The shop accepts donations of used books, resells them, and uses the profits to support its programs. The organization is housed in the Brownhoist, a beautiful historic office building now home to the arts.

### 77 SECOND CHANCE BOOK NOOK............................. 44

**East Liverpool**

This used bookstore partners with The Way Station, a community center that helps people in need with everything from job-readiness classes to food distribution. People who purchase books at the bookstore help fund these programs.

**78 SERENITY BOOK SHOP** ....... 45

**Columbus**

Serenity's owner set out to provide a healing and calming space for readers. Patrons are welcome to read, work, or study with relaxing music.

**79 (THE) OHIO BOOK STORE** .. 45

**Cincinnati**

In 84 years, this establishment has expanded its size, its stock, and its services to become one of the oldest, biggest, and best of Ohio's bookstores.

**80 VISIBLE VOICE BOOKS** ........ 45

**Cleveland**

At this bookstore, you can not only find the perfect read but also sip a glass of wine or a cup of coffee while you browse.

**81 WHEATBERRY BOOKS** ........ 45

**Chillicothe**

This charming bookstore is located in historic downtown Chillicothe. The hardwood floors, rugs, and reading chairs make it perfect for relaxing and reading a good book before buying one.

**In 2020, The Ohioana Library Association created The Ohio Literary Trail, which includes many literary landmarks and destinations across the state.**

*Find out more about*

# BOOKS, BOOKS & MORE BOOKS

## 43 APPLETREE BOOKS

**12419 Cedar Road,
Cleveland Heights, OH 44106
216-791-2665
appletree-books.com**

At Appletree, located in the Heights Center, the staff likes to recommend books that transport readers to other places. They're also pleased to sell gift and stationery items.

## 44 BEANBAG BOOKS

**25 West Winter Street,
Delaware, OH 43015; 740-363-0290
beanbagbooks.com**

The folks at Beanbag Books love kids, families, books, beanbags, and inclusivity. There are five book clubs here, plus a full schedule of events for children and adults.

## 45 BIRCH TREE BOOKERY

**605 East Center Sreet, Suite B,
Marion, OH 43302; 740-262-3312
facebook.com/birchtreebookery**

Birch Tree loves to bring book lovers together via a friendly atmosphere, book clubs, and community events. Used books are available in all genres, as well as toys, games, jewelry, and home decor.

## 46 THE BOOK LOFT

**631 South Third Street,
Columbus, OH 43206, and
632 City Park Avenue,
Columbus, OH 43206; 614-464-1774
bookloft.com**

This is one of the largest independent bookstores in the United States. Its 32 rooms have grown organically since 1977, gradually taking over pre-Civil War buildings that housed stores, a nickelodeon, and a saloon. The current structure stretches through a city block between South Third Street and City Park Avenue. (It's often easier to find parking on City Park Avenue.)

The store is a delightfully crowded hodgepodge of books, calendars, puzzles, cards, accessories, and more books. Every fiction genre you can think of is here, from science fiction to romance and from hard-boiled crime to cozy mystery. Every nonfiction category is here, too, from psychology to parapsychology and from gardening to bugs. Plan on spending several hours and getting lost at least twice.

## 47 BOOKERY CINCY

**3704 Eastern Avenue,
Cincinnati, OH 45226; 513-818-8088
bookerycincy.com**

The owners don't have anything against technology, but they feel that scrolling and TV bingeing are stealing time from reading. Thus, the Bookery is a place where people can discover, or rediscover, the irresistible magic found between the pages of books.

## 48 BOOKMARX BOOKSTORE

**181 North 4th Street,
Steubenville, OH 43952;
740-282-6100
bookmarxbooks.com**

If your interests sometimes take a left turn from bestsellers to delve into vintage and classic books, you'll have a grand time at BookMarx. Here, you can find titles like *Alice in Wonderland, Beowulf,* and *Dickens' Stories about Children*. There's always a good selection of books by Tolkien, C.S. Lewis, G.K. Chesterton, and George MacDonald. You'll find a growing collection of Greek and Latin classics. In the local interest section, you can browse books by local authors as well as books on the Ohio Valley. There's even a selection of books curated by Raven, the resident feline, including *A Hiss before Dying* and *The Domestic Cat in Roman Civilization*.

## 49 BOOKS IN STOCK

**140 East Liberty Street,**
**Wooster, OH 44691; 330-262-2665**
**booksinstock.net**

Used and rare books are the specialties here, where buy-sell-trade customers are welcome. Tens of thousands of books are sorted and carefully stocked in this spacious store.

## 50 THE BOOKSHELF

**7754 Camargo Road,**
**Madeira, OH 45243; 513-271-9140**
**cincybookshelf.com**

After 48 years, these booksellers know what they like and, more importantly, what their customers and book club members like. Even their dog, Charley, has some favorite picks.

## 51 BUCKEYE BOOK FAIR

**527 North Market Street, Suite 2,**
**Wooster, OH 44691; 330-249-1455**
**buckeyebookfair.org**

Do you love books? Do you love meeting the authors and illustrators who produce them? Come to the Buckeye Book Fair. The primary mission of the long-running event is to promote literacy and support Ohio authors and illustrators of all ages. The fair itself happens on an early November Saturday and is preceded by a student literacy day, a young authors' conference, and a Buckeye Book Crawl through downtown Wooster featuring authors' programs at different locales. Dozens of Ohio authors and illustrators will be present when the fair opens, signing and selling their books. Throughout the rest of the year, the organization supports students, teachers, and librarians.

## 52 CINCY BOOK BUS DEPOT

**10936 Reading Road,**
**Sharonville, OH 45241**
**the-book-bus.square.site**

Former teacher Melanie Moore drives an adorable mint-green 1962 VW truck from the Book Bus Depot to cruise Cincinnati, bringing books to book lovers. A portion of her profits and her time provides books to low-income schools.

## 53 COLUMBUS BOOK FESTIVAL

**Main Library and Topiary Park,**
**96 South Grant Avenue,**
**Columbus, OH 43215; 614-645-2275**
**columbusbookfestival.org**

This is a new addition to the Ohio festival lineup, committed to celebrating the community of book lovers. More than 200 authors bring their books to the festival to sign and sell. During the two-day summer event, there are author talks and panel discussions in the library, as well as author stages outside in Topiary Park. Also outdoors are exhibitor tents, family activities, and food trucks galore. You can find a gift for a reader at the merchandise tables and browse through

Indie Author Alley. The Friends of the Library have their own book sale tent.

## 54 COVER TO COVER: BOOKS FOR YOUNG READERS

**2116 Arlington Avenue, Columbus, OH 43221; 614-263-1624**
**covertocoverchildrensbooks.com**

For more than 40 years, Cover to Cover has served not only children and young adults but also educators, librarians, and parents. Scavenger hunts, author events, and summer reading events are popular here.

## 55 DARK STAR BOOKS

**237 Xenia Avenue, Suite B, Yellow Springs, OH 45387-1875**
**937-767-9400**
**darkstarbookstore.com**

It started out by selling comics, but it wasn't long before Dark Star blossomed into a full-service bookstore while maintaining thousands of vintage comic books. The shelves are overflowing with books and Geek Culture collectibles.

## 56 DOWNBOUND BOOKS

**4139 Apple Street, Cincinnati, OH 45223; 513-541-1394**
**downboundbooks.com**

At Downbound, a small but picturesque neighborhood establishment, the books tend to be those that aren't readily found elsewhere. Besides bestsellers and children's books, there is a good selection of Indigenous and trans literature.

The owners also have a sense of humor. Their categories include Forage, Find, Feast; Work, Work, Work; Sweet Teeth; Tales Retold; Grown-Up Graphica; and Delightful Reads for Summertime Needs.

## 57 ELIZABETH'S BOOKSHOP & WRITING CENTRE

**647 East Market Street, Unit 3, Akron, OH 44304; 330-815-1285**
**elizabethsofakronshop.com**

Owner Rachel Cargle donates part of her profits to the Loveland Corporation Inc, which offers free therapy to Black women and girls, and people of nonconforming gender. She also runs a writing center for both writers and readers in the community. Workshops, readings, and events like book signings and meetups are offered. Elizabeth's also supports teachers with discounts, exclusive events, free field trips, and school fundraising opportunities.

Staff picks for favorite books range from *The Hunger Games* to *Quilting Poems* to *The Late Homecoming: A Hmong Family Memoir.*

## 58 EPIC BOOK SHOP

**232 Xenia Avenue, Yellow Springs, OH 45387**
**937-767-2091**
**epic-bookshop.com**

Offering new and used books, Epic has been in business for more than 50 years. Their children's section includes books on kid yoga, history, and classics, as well as nesting dolls, board games, and puzzles. On the spiritual side for adults, books are available on the occult, Wicca, healing, folklore, and reincarnation.

## 59 FAITH VIEW BOOKS

**4964 Township Road 616, Fredericksburg, OH 44627**
**330-674-0684**
**facebook.com/faithviewbooks**

This sprawling Amish store sits grandly in the middle of farm country on a quiet back road. The long front porch is filled with benches and rockers that are just right for visiting friends and browsing new purchases while you enjoy your favorite coffee or tea from the café inside. The book selections include true stories, children's books, Bibles, and other Christian nonfiction. There's also a large adult fiction section that includes tales with Amish themes. Faith View has many things to offer besides books. There are irresistible gift items; a wall of music CDs and movies; plus clothing, purses, and totes. The staff is friendly and welcoming and happy to serve visitors.

## 60 THE FINE PRINT BOOKSHOP

**202 Walnut Avenue,**
**Lakeside-Marblehead, OH 43440**
**419-702-7064**
**facebook.com/thefineprintlksd**

The cozy establishment welcomes children with scavenger hunts and storytimes that have special themes. They even sell toys to go along with the books the kids choose. Older kids have been known to come to their favorite place for prom photos. Adult patrons can shop for books that have been chosen by local book clubs and book review groups.

## 61 FIRESIDE BOOKSHOP

**29 North Franklin Street,**
**Chagrin Falls, OH 44022**
**440-247-4050**
**firesidebookshop.com**

Fireside has been open to book lovers since 1963. Three floors of new and gently used books entice both longtime and new patrons to stop in and stay awhile. If you like dogs as well as you like books, look around for Zolla, an Icelandic sheepdog who has definite opinions on which books people should read. Fireside keeps a stock of books required for reading at local schools, including classics like *The Crucible* and *The Catcher in the Rye.* The third-floor children's section includes an entire room where preschoolers can browse and play. The little ones even have their own subscription book program, ensuring each child receives a new gift-wrapped book in the mail every month. For adults, you can't go wrong with the helpful and enticing staff picks. There are also frequent book-signing events.

## 62 FOX'S BOOK ADVENTURES

**12793 State Route 664 South,**
**Logan, OH 43138; 740-385-0400**
**foxsbookadventures.com**

Inside Treehouse Treats and Treasures candy-and-ice-cream store, you'll find this small and intriguing bookstore. Fox's carries children's and young adult books; adult fiction and nonfiction; and toys, games, and gifts.

## 63 GODDESS ELITE

**28887 Lorain Road,**
**North Olmsted, OH 44070**
**440-777-7211**
**goddesselite.com**

Goddess Elite started out as a New Age gift shop that also offered metaphysical gifts and services. They continue that tradition today, adding books that focus on spiritual healing, tarot, and spell casting. In addition, they offer Reiki, astrological charting, singing bowl concerts, and haunted outings, among other things. Also, at Goddess Elite, shoppers who live far away from the store or would rather shop from home can opt for a virtual personal shopping appointment. The cost of the appointment is then applied to whatever the shopper buys from the selections offered.

## 64 GRAMERCY BOOKS

**2424 East Main Street, Bexley, OH 43209; 614-867-5515**
**gramercybooksbexley.com**

Gramercy offers a Bookgram option to readers, sending a book in your favorite genre to your home every other month. It also offers a frequent-buyer program, book discussions, and author events.

## 65 HOLLY'S BOOK RACK

**2180 West Fourth Street, Ontario, OH 44906; 419-756-2667**
**advkeen.co/holly_bkrack**

The long, long rows of book racks draw shoppers in at Holly's. You can find new and used books here, nicely organized and priced affordably. They also sell audiobooks and reading accessories. They trade more than 300 titles per day and are committed to offering respect, courtesy, and honesty to their customers.

## 66 JOSEPH-BETH BOOKSELLERS

**2692 Madison Road, Suite M, Cincinnati, OH 45208; 513-396-8960**
**josephbeth.com**

The frequent programs offered at Joseph-Beth include book signings, discussions, presentations by creative writing students, book club meetings, and crafts nights. A summer program for children highlights books and graphic novels. Periodic book fairs offer discounts to students and their families. Their Educators Resource Network provides offers and programming exclusively for teachers.

The wide variety of books for sale includes dozens of fiction genres and nonfiction categories. Frequent shoppers can join a rewards program that offers member-only discounts, events, and offers.

## 67 KICKS MIX BOOKSTORE

**38 South Third Street, Newark, OH 43055**
**740-345-9800**
**kicksmixbookstore.com**

New and used books, a friendly staff, and the occasional cat make this small neighborhood shop inviting. It has a little of everything, from bestsellers to comic books.

## 68 THE LEARNED OWL BOOK SHOP

**204 North Main Street, Hudson, OH 44236**
**330-653-2252 or 800-968-2685**
**learnedowl.com**

Books are stacked everywhere here–in the bookshelves, on freestanding racks, at the sides of the stair treads, and up to the ceilings. It almost makes you want to hide somewhere and get locked in for the night.

The Learned Owl is proud to have hosted hundreds of book and author events over the past 50 years, and the store is very willing to support local authors. For readers, it hosts two local book clubs, and of course there are all those books to browse. Customers can access up to 100,000 audiobooks through an online service.

## 69 LITTLE SPARROW BOOKSHOP

**1200 North Main Street, North Canton, OH 44720**
**330-967-2142**
**littlesparrowbooks.com**

THE SECOND FLOOR OF A LARGE USED BOOK STORE IN OHIO

This woman-owned independent bookstore sells new and used books, as well as collectible and special-edition books. Author events, book clubs, and holiday celebrations are some of their offerings.

## 70 LOGANBERRY BOOKS

**13015 Larchmere Boulevard, Shaker Heights, OH 44120**
**216-795-9800**
**loganberrybooks.com**

The very coolest thing about Loganberry Books is the Book Spine Mural on the side of the building. It was erected in 2011 as part of a public art project, and the books represented are children's literature and books about the surrounding community and its businesses.

Loganberry is a busy place, with a calendar full of book signings, art receptions, children's activities, poetry and performance events, reading challenges, and even a monthly hybrid yoga class/ book club. In its gifts department, Loganberry offers mystery grab bags at different price levels and book bundles that are grouped by genre. The store supports authors in the community with its Local Voices Program and with an annual book festival, Author Alley, in August.

## 71 MAC'S BACKS-BOOKS ON COVENTRY

**1820 Coventry Road, Cleveland Heights, OH 44118**
**216-321-2665**
**macsbacks.com**

Three floors of new and used books await readers here. There are regular poetry readings, book club meetings, author signings, and musical events.

## 72 NEW AND OLD PAGES BOOK SHOPPE

**856 Union Boulevard, Englewood, OH 45322**
**937-832-3022**
**advkeen.co/new_olde**

You can find a wide variety of new and used books here, but the specialties are military and history titles. Story times, author events, and holiday celebrations are on the calendar at New and Old Pages.

## 73 OHIOANA BOOK FESTIVAL

**Festival location:**
**Columbus Metropolitan Library, 96 South Grant Avenue, Columbus, OH 43215**
**Ohioana Library:**
**274 East First Avenue, Suite 300, Columbus, OH 43201; 614-466-3831**
**ohioana.org/programs/ohioana-book-festival**

It happens once a year, on a Saturday in April, and it's free. Ohioana Festival is paradise for a book lover, since more than 100 Ohio writers set up shop to sell their wares. You can find everything from history to children's fantasy here, plus all there is in between. There are panel discussions, food trucks, book-signing events, and activities for children and teens. For educators, librarians, and workshop directors, the Ohioana Library also provides a directory of authors available for appearances all year long.

## 74 PARAGRAPHS BOOKSTORE

**229 South Main Street, Mount Vernon, OH 43050**
**740-392-9290**
**paragraphsbookstore.com**

Paragraphs is a charming bookstore with a set-back front on Main Street. Chairs inside and out invite browsers to settle in and sample a book or two at their leisure.

The staff picks here cut a wide swath through multiple genres in old as well as new books. Are you in the mood for science fiction? The staff can recommend some of those. Do you read mostly nonfiction? They've got you covered there too. Or do you prefer classics–old books that you read as a child and would love to rediscover? They'll point you toward some of their favorites.

## 75 PROLOGUE BOOKSHOP

**841 North High Street, Columbus, OH 43215**
**614-745-1395**
**prologuebookshop.com**

The next time you're enjoying the Short North District of Columbus, stop by the Prologue Bookshop, proud to be an independent business and to keep profits in the community.

## 76 THE READING ROOM

**The Brownhoist, 4403 St. Clair Avenue, 3rd Floor, Cleveland, OH 44103**
**216-200-7723**
**readingroomcle.org**

The Reading Room, housed in an arts center, is a nonprofit bookstore supporting literacy and literary programs. Donated books are accepted for resale.

## 77 SECOND CHANCE BOOK NOOK

**135 West 5th Street, East Liverpool, OH 43920**
**304-479-4060**
**advkeen.co/way_station**

Used books fight for space at the non-profit Book Nook, a tiny and friendly two-room storefront that carries a wide range of adult fiction and nonfiction, children's and young adult books, Christian books, and free Bibles. The store is staffed by volunteers, and 100% of the profits support The Way Station, a community resource center next door.

## 78 SERENITY BOOK SHOP

**1806 West 5th Avenue,**
**Columbus, OH 43212**
**614-525-0506**
**serenitybookshop.com**

Serenity's owner calls this an all-you-need bookshop. Her goal is to provide a welcoming and relaxing atmosphere that feeds the soul. One of her new initiatives is called Sip and Shop, for which patrons choose a beverage and enjoy an evening with books. A 10% discount makes the event even more enjoyable.

There are some surprising and far-ranging books on the shelves, like *The Backyard Bird Chronicles* for bird lovers, written and illustrated by Amy Tan; *The Ministry of Time,* a science fiction novel; *Who is Taylor Swift?* for the kids; and *In My Time of Dying,* a reflection on mortality and the afterlife.

## 79 (THE) OHIO BOOK STORE

**726 Main Street,**
**Cincinnati, OH 45202**
**513-621-5142**
**ohiobookstore.net**

Can you even imagine five stories of books? Of course you can—and you probably can't wait to go there. The Ohio Book Store was founded in 1940, and the current owner has been there since 1956. The massive store holds 300,000 used books and magazines, so be sure to allow several hours for browsing. If you allowed several days, you still might not see it all.

## 80 VISIBLE VOICE BOOKS

**2258 Professor Avenue,**
**Cleveland, OH 44113**
**216-961-0084**
**visiblevoicebooks.com**

Fun-seeking book lovers can get together and schedule a Brunch and Browse at Visible Voice. The event includes coffee, tea, mimosas, pastries, and a merchandise credit, plus 90 exclusive minutes for your group to browse the bookstore. You can do the same thing at an evening Create Your Own Night party. Dinner from a local pizza shop, plus a bottle of wine, pairs nicely with 100 minutes of exclusive book browsing and a merchandise credit. The store's café offers coffee, tea, cocoa, a rotating selection of wine and beer, plus goodies that include Cleveland Chocolate Co. candy bars. Visible Voice also stocks its calendar with book and author events, live music, discussion groups, meetups, and wine and beer tastings.

## 81 WHEATBERRY BOOKS

**9 West 2nd Street,**
**Chillicothe, OH 45601; 740-771-3369**
**wheatberrybooks.com**

Wheatberry's has both a fiction and a nonfiction book club, and members get a 15% discount on books. New and used books are available here, for both adults and children.

HIKERS AT BUZZARDROOST ROCK, EDGE OF APPALACHIA PRESERVE SYSTEM, SOUTHERN OHIO

**When the last leaf and the first snowflake have fallen, Ohioans begin to think about winter activities.**

There's always curling up in front of the fireplace with a good book, but more vigorous activity is good too. You can check out the downhill skiing in northern Ohio or the cross-country skiing through state forests and parks. Some areas have snowmobile trails. You can go ice fishing on the lakes, and you can even watch a dogsled race, weather permitting.

*Welcome to*

# ENJOYING THE SNOW

*Find out more about*

# ENJOYING THE SNOW

## 82 BOSTON MILLS/ BRANDYWINE SKI RESORTS

7100 Riverview Road,
Peninsula, OH 44264-0175
330-657-2334
bmbw.com

These side-by-side resorts open for the winter ski season as soon as snow—natural or man-made—is available. If you've never tried skiing or snowboarding, these resorts make it easy for you to get started. You can rent any equipment you need, get lift tickets, then sign up for a group class or private lessons. If you don't want to go down the mountain on your feet, they've got that covered, too, at the Polar Blast tubing area at Brandywine. All you have to do is jump on a snow tube and head down the tubing lanes. There are even conveyor lifts to carry you back up the hill, and you can take a break in the lodge for hot cocoa and snacks.

## 83 CROSS-COUNTRY SKIING, SNOWSHOEING & SNOWMOBILING

### CLEVELAND METROPARKS

**83A Big Met Golf Course**
4811 Valley Parkway,
Fairview Park, OH 44126
440-331-1070
For ski conditions: 216-635-3270
advkeen.co/winter_activities

### LAKE METROPARKS

For equipment rentals: 440-256-3810

**83B Chapin Forest Reservation**
9938 Chillicothe Road,
Kirtland, OH 44094; 440-358-7275

**83C Girdled Road Reservation**
12926 Radcliffe Road,
Concord Township, 44077

**83D Penitentiary Glen Reservation**
8668 Kirtland Chardon Road,
Willoughby, OH 44094
440-256-1404
lakemetroparks.com/events-activities/activities/cross-country-skiing-snowshoeing

### SNOWMOBILING

**83E Buck Creek State Park**
1976 Buck Creek Lane,
Springfield, OH 45502
937-322-5284
ohiodnr.gov/go-and-do/plan-a-visit/find-a-property/buck-creek-state-park

**83F Mosquito Lake State Park**
OH 305, Cortland, OH 44410
330-637-2856
ohiodnr.gov/go-and-do/plan-a-visit/find-a-property/mosquito-lake-state-park

**83G West Branch State Park**
5570 Esworthy Road,
Ravenna, OH 44266
330-235-0030
ohiodnr.gov/go-and-do/plan-a-visit/find-a-property/west-branch-state-park

**83H Western Reserve Greenway**
West 52nd Street and
Madison Avenue (Ashtabula)
and North River Road (Warren)
advkeen.co/western_reserve

## 84 ICE MAN GUIDE SERVICE

**Office: 165 Benedict Avenue, Norwalk, OH 44857; 419-341-9721**
**advkeen.co/put-in-bay**

If you're a die-hard fan of fishing who doesn't mind a little cold weather, this guide service will get you through the winter, with experienced, licensed guides and all the equipment you need for a comfortable ice fishing experience. Pickups are available in Port Clinton, or you can fly to Put-in-Bay. Up to 36 people per day can be transported to heated ice shanties. Tackle is provided, and guides drill the holes and provide lunch.

## 85 MAD RIVER MOUNTAIN

**1000 Snow Valley Road, Zanesfield, OH 43360**
**937-599-1015 or 800-231-7669**
**skimadriver.com**

Snow tubing at Bubly Tubing Park is popular at Mad River Mountain. Besides the tubing lanes, there are two conveyor belt lifts, a lodge, and an outdoor fire pit. With a mountain full of trails and four terrain parks, skiing at Mad River provides hours of fun. There are ski schools for groups and individuals, plus plenty of help for first-timers. College ID Nights during the season feature special rates for students. There are also homeschool days and Scout days. Racing and development programs are offered to young athletes.

## 86 PUNDERSON SLED DOG CLASSIC

**Punderson State Park, 11755 Kinsman Road, Newbury Township, OH 44065**
**440-564-2279**
**advkeen.co/punderson_sled_dog**
**advkeen.co/sled_dog_race**

Because this event (also known as the Great Sled Dog Race Classic of Northeast Ohio) takes place in Ohio, it doesn't happen every year. The Siberian Husky Club of Greater Cleveland schedules a race date plus an alternate date every winter, but sometimes there just isn't enough of a good snow base at Punderson. Still, when the event happens, it's great winter entertainment. There are dogsled races in several classes, plus a skijoring race. (In skijoring, an individual dog pulls its owner along on skis.) You'll see beautifully matched teams of purebred Siberian Huskies or Alaskan Malamutes, as well as open classes for mixed teams of eager scrappers. No matter their pedigree, the dogs are always wildly excited, howling in their traces, eager to run. On the starter's signal, the dogs leap into action, and the race is on. As long as it snows, of course.

## 87 SNOW TRAILS SKI RESORT

**3100 Possum Run Road, Mansfield, OH 44903; 419-774-9818 or 800-OHIO-SKI (800-644-6754)**
**snowtrails.com**

Open for skiing and tubing mid-December through mid-March, weather permitting, Snow Trails has multiple downhill runs and lifts, and four terrain parks, built from scratch every winter. There are also six 1,100-foot tubing runs with conveyor lifts. For extra fun, try nighttime Glow Tubing. The Tubing Lodge has a snack bar and outdoor fire pit. There are several places to find food and drink at Snow Trails, including the Last Run Bar and Deli and Lucky's Cafeteria. Private, semiprivate, group, children's, and women-only lessons are available. An adaptive ski program accommodates skiers with disabilities. In the off-season, the 215-seat day lodge and 85-seat Valley Lodge are available for rental. Outdoor events take place at the base of the slopes.

FERRIS WHEEL DETAIL AT THE OHIO STATE FAIR

**Whether your tastes run to music, Renaissance history, or hot-air balloons, there's a festival somewhere in Ohio just for you.**

Wear comfortable shoes, take some cash for the food trucks, and spend a day—or more—soaking up the festival vibes.

**88 CINCINNATI ZOO FESTIVAL OF LIGHTS** .......... 53

**Cincinnati**

For more than 30 years, the zoo has turned its grounds into a Wild Wonderland with more than 2 million holiday lights November through January.

**89 COUNTRY CONCERT** .......... 53

**Fort Laramie**

Since 1981, the Country Concert has welcomed music lovers to this three-day event. Four stages and nine giant screens ensure no one misses a thing.

**90 GREAT TRAIL ARTS & CRAFTS FESTIVAL** .......... 53

**Malvern**

This long-running event, held over two late-summer weekends, celebrates folk art and the French and Indian era of early American history.

**91 HOT-AIR BALLOON FESTIVALS** .......... 53

**Statewide**

There's nothing quite like watching a hot-air balloon rise over the horizon. Imagine a whole sky filled with them.

**92 MADE IN OHIO ART & CRAFT FESTIVAL** .......... 54

**Bath**

This two-day juried festival at Hale Farm & Village attracts more than 120 artisans selling everything from pottery and jewelry to soaps and woodcarvings, all made in Ohio.

**93 OHIO RENAISSANCE FESTIVAL** .......... 54

**Waynesville**

Jousts and swordfights, strolling minstrels, magicians, and puppeteers provide continuous entertainment, and visitors are invited to test their strength, storm the castle, learn archery, or try out the throwing axes and knives.

**94 OHIO RIVER STERNWHEEL FESTIVAL** .......... 55

**Marietta**

Always held the weekend after Labor Day, the Sternwheel Festival can attract more than 100,000 people to enjoy authentic sternwheelers as well as family entertainment and activities.

**95 SHAKER WOODS FESTIVALS** .......... 55

**Columbiana**

There really are woods. The wooded area behind a farm field is used three times a year: for the original Shaker Woods Crafters and Artisans Festival, featuring juried arts and crafts, Antiques in the Woods, and Christmas in the Woods.

**The international Twins Festival is held yearly in Twinsburg, Ohio.**

HOT AIR BALLOON FESTIVAL, COSHOCTON

## *Find out more about* FESTIVALS

### 88 CINCINNATI ZOO FESTIVAL OF LIGHTS

**3400 Vine Street, Cincinnati, OH 45220; 513-281-4700**
**advkeen.co/fest_lights**

The holidays arrive at the zoo via the lighted North Polar Express Train, the Conservation Carousel, and more than 4 million lights. Strolling entertainers roam the zoo through themed areas, like Santa's Village and Fairyland where there are five hidden Fiona fairies. Santa and Mrs. Claus are available for visits. A Wild Lights show is offered at Swan Lake, and there's a black-light Madcap Puppets show. Two S'mores-N-More stands are on the grounds, along with other holiday fare. After Christmas, a Happy ZOO Year party is held December 31. The festival runs from mid-November through early January.

### 89 COUNTRY CONCERT

**7103 State Route 66, Fort Loramie, OH 45845**
**937-295-3000**
**countryconcert.com**

Not only can you hear great country music stars, you can be one yourself, on Karaoke Night at the long-running midsummer Country Concert. There are two ways to enjoy the long weekend of entertainment. Order a hotel/bus package and catered meals delivered to your VIP seats; or sleep in your own camper, tent, or rental RV and carry your own food and drinks to seating on the grass. Either way, you'll have a great time dancing and singing along to nonstop music.

### 90 GREAT TRAIL ARTS & CRAFTS FESTIVAL

**6331 Canton Road Northwest, Malvern, OH 44644**
**330-794-9100**
**greattrailfestival.com**

Great Trail is a celebration of Colonial America, with plenty of history on display. There are lectures and demonstrations each day, as well as rendezvous and battle reenactments. The Ohio State tomahawk-throwing contest is part of the action. Entertainment includes flag raisings and parades, fiddlers, cloggers, bands, and pipers. A bison herd, including a white calf born there, is on display at the grounds, as is a scenic gristmill. Crafters who attend for demonstrations and sales include candlemakers, wicker furniture makers, birdhouse builders, soap makers, potters, blacksmiths, and basket makers. There's also a popular Baker's Row.

### 91 HOT-AIR BALLOON FESTIVALS

**Statewide**

#### 91A All Ohio Balloon Fest

**Union County Airport, 760 Clymer Road, Marysville, OH 43040; 937-243-5833**
**allohioballoonfest.com**

#### 91B Ashland Balloon Fest

**Free Field, 1256 Center Street, Ashland, OH 44805**
**419-281-4584 ext. 101 or 877-581-2345 ext. 101**
**ashlandohioballoonfest.com**

### 91C Balloons Over Wadsworth

Wadsworth Municipal Airport,
840 Airport Drive,
Wadsworth, OH 44281; 330-336-6150
balloonsoverwadsworth.com

### 91D Coshocton Hot Air Balloon Festival

Coshocton County Fairgrounds,
707 Kenilworth Avenue,
Coshocton, OH 43812
740-622-2385
coshoctonhotairballoonfestival.com

### 91E Defiance County Hot Air Balloon Festival

Defiance County Airport,
20399 Airport Road,
Defiance, OH 43512; 419-782-3510
defianceballoonfest.com

### 91F Flag City Balloon Fest

Emory Adams Park,
1827 South Blanchard Street,
Findlay, OH 45840
419-422-3313
flagcityballoonfest.com

### 91G Montpelier Bean Days Hot Air Balloon Fest

Williams County Fairgrounds,
619 East Main Street,
Montpelier, OH 43543; 419-485-4416
advkeen.co/montpelier_balloon

### 91H Ohio Challenge

Smith Park,
500-546 Tytus Avenue,
Middletown, OH 45042; 513-422-4551
ohiochallenge.com

### 91I Pro Football Hall of Fame Enshrinement Festival Balloon Classic & Fireworks

Kent State University, Stark Campus,
6000 Frank Avenue Northwest,
North Canton, OH 44720
30-456-7253
advkeen.co/balloon_classic

### 91J Ravenna Balloon A Fair

Sunbeau Valley Farm,
3229 OH-59, Ravenna OH 44266
330-296-3247
ravennaballoonafair.com

## 92 MADE IN OHIO ART & CRAFT FESTIVAL

Hale Farm & Village,
2686 Oak Hill Road, Bath, OH 44210
330-666-3711
madeinohiofestival.org

Every September, Hale Farm & Village hosts this juried festival of handmade and homegrown products for more than 12,000 visitors. Artisans include woodcarvers, glass and jewelry makers, quilters, artists, potters, and makers of soaps and lotions. Local vintners and brewers are also on hand, plus food vendors. Musical entertainment is provided, and costumed docents are on call throughout the village. (See also Hale Farm and Village, page 56.)

## 93 OHIO RENAISSANCE FESTIVAL

10542 East State Route 73,
Waynesville, OH 45068; 513-897-7000
renfestival.com

On the grounds of a 30-acre 16th-century replica English village, visitors are welcome to attend the Ohio Renaissance Festival on nine weekends in September and October. Each weekend has its own theme. On the Feast of Fools Weekend you'll get a bellyful of laughs, tricks, and a Pumpkin vs. Watermelon War that signals the change of seasons. Traditional Scottish games and music are featured on Highland Weekend, or show your witchy side on Fantasy

Weekend. Renew your wedding vows with other starry-eyed couples on Romance Weekend. More than 100 entertainers roam the festival grounds, from acrobats and jugglers to harpists and bagpipers. Sixteenth-century food is available in abundance, like soup in bread bowls, haggis, and a pickle cart, plus more ordinary fare, including ice cream and pizza. Handmade crafts, jewelry, and clothing are sold in the Artisan Marketplace.

## 94 OHIO RIVER STERNWHEEL FESTIVAL

**119 Greene Street,**
**Marietta, OH 45750; 740-373-5178**
**ohioriversternwheelfestival.org**

Sternwheeler racing used to be a regular sight along the Ohio River. This festival preserves the tradition. Thousands cheer the boats upriver as whistles blow and captains jockey for position. Other events include the crowning of Queen Genevieve and the Little Miss and Mister, fireworks, a car show, photo contest, and the Sternwheel 5K run and walk. There are also children's activities and musical entertainment.

## 95 SHAKER WOODS FESTIVALS

**44337 County Line Road,**
**Columbiana, OH 44408; 330-482-0214**
**shakerwoods.com**
**christmasinthewoodsohio.com**
**advkeen.co/antiques**

In the woods behind a farm field off Route 7, four different events make up the Shaker Woods family of festivals. The original Shaker Woods Festival is held over three weekends every August, featuring more than 200 juried craftspeople and artists. Antiques in the Woods is always on a September weekend, featuring dealers in quality antiques and collectibles. The newest event, Shaker Woods Outdoor Expo, takes place at the same time. Outdoor adventurers are invited to meet vendors to learn about hunting, fishing, camping, outdoor art, and outdoor sports. At Christmas in the Woods, during two weekends in October, visitors shop for handcrafted Christmas gifts. All the events include food vendors, themed entertainment, and sometimes extra activities, like poker runs and antique car displays.

OHIO RIVER STERNWHEEL FESTIVAL, MARIETTA

DIAMONDBACK ROLLER COASTER, KINGS ISLAND

## There's plenty of fun to be had in Ohio.

Do you like roller coasters? We've got that covered. Does your idea of a day trip mean a visit to Amish country for shopping and great food? Just head to southern Ohio. Are you a fan of merry-go-rounds? Visit the Richland Carrousel Park in Mansfield and choose your ride. Whatever tickles your fancy, you'll find a trip that fits.

Welcome to

# FUN GETAWAYS

**The first roller coaster at Cedar Point was built in 1892. It stood 25 feet tall and reached a whopping top speed of 10 miles per hour.**

## *Find out more about*
## FUN GETAWAYS

### 96 AKRON ZOO

**505 Euclid Avenue, Akron, OH 44307**
**330-375-2550**
**akronzoo.org**

Pandas and pythons and penguins; lemurs, leopards, lions, and lorises; seahorses and snakes and storks: all you can say is, "Oh, my!"

Diversity is important at the Akron Zoo, and not just among animals. Both guests and employees are diverse as well. The zoo has been given an Age-Friendly Seal of Approval designation. There are accessible pathways and trains throughout. Service animals that meet ADA Title III regulations are welcome. Wheelchairs are free, and strollers and fanciful electric scooters can be rented. A sensory inclusion program offers weighted pads, earphones, and other items. There are quiet zones and a comfort station. The zoo also has Dementia Friends certification.

Zoo tours begin early with a Rise-and-Shine Safari. Later you can tour Behind-the-Scenes and Get-Closer with Galapagos turtles and other animals. And as if that weren't enough, the zoo also offers education programs for children and families.

### 97 AMISH COUNTRY

**Holmes County Chamber of Commerce & Tourism Bureau,**
**6 West Jackson Street,**
**Millersburg, OH 44654**
**330-674-3975**
**visitamishcountry.com**

It might be a yearning for a simpler time, or it might be that we admire them for their refusal to embrace most modern technology, but whatever the reason, Amish people and their lifestyle fascinate us. Ohioans have plenty of opportunities to be impressed, especially in the southeast, where Amish and Mennonite farms and businesses are spread over five counties. The best spot in Amish country, many people believe, is Lehman's Hardware Store in Dalton. If you're in the market for a natural peanut butter stirrer, a mill to grind your own flour, or blueprints for building a windmill, this is the place to look. But don't stop there. Elsewhere in Amish country, attend a play; tour a farm; or browse through a bookstore, a quilt shop, or a store filled with handmade furniture. Buy some cheese, try some baked goods, and, by all means, sit down at a family-style Amish restaurant.

## 98 CEDAR POINT AMUSEMENT PARK

**1 Cedar Point Drive,
Sandusky, OH 44870; 419-627-2350
cedarpoint.com**

For families in search of sun and fun, this is the place to go in Ohio. More than 3 million people visit the roller-coaster capital of the world each season. The Top Thrill 2, launched in 2024, is the new, tallest, and fastest triple-launch strata roller coaster in the world. Don't forget, though, there are 17 other coasters, including the venerable Wild Mouse. There are dozens of other rides, places to eat, and arcades.

The rides are just for openers, though. At Cedar Point Beach you can chill out, ride a waverunner, or go parasailing. Boardwalk Nights at the beach offers food and drink, music and lights, dancing, live shows, and family games. You can even enjoy a guided morning tour in a pedicab, complete with mimosas and pastries. Afternoon and evening tours feature either wine or beer, snacks, and a souvenir.

At Cedar Point's 18-acre waterpark, brave visitors can take a six-story plunge down Point Plummet. The less brave can try other slides, rapids, and raceways, or hang out with the kids at Lemmy's Lagoon or the Lily Pad Walk.

## 99 COLUMBUS ZOO & AQUARIUM

**4850 West Powell Road,
Powell, OH 43065; 614-645-3400
columbuszoo.org**

People all over the world know about the Columbus Zoo, thanks to its former director and director emeritus, Jack Hanna. Besides the usual lions, tigers, and bears, the zoo's 7,000-plus residents include sea lions, giraffes, Asian elephants, Tasmanian devils, and koalas, but I have to say the Pallas' cat is my favorite. Programs at the zoo are inventive and fun. You can help give an elephant a bath, take a night hike, feed a stingray, have an up-close wild encounter, or meet a reindeer. One of the unique programs at the zoo is Outreach, which provides animals, handlers, and speakers for schools, senior citizen facilities, and events as small as a birthday party or as large as a corporate conference. The facility also includes the nearby amusement park Jungle Jack's Landing, the Zoombezi Bay Water Park, and The Wilds conservation center in Cumberland (see page 150).

## 100 HARTVILLE MARKETPLACE & FLEA MARKET

**1289 Edison Street Northwest,
Hartville, OH 44632; 330-877-9860
hartvillemarketplace.com**

When Sol Miller started a livestock auction in 1939, it didn't take long to add an egg auction, rent outdoor space to vendors, and put in a lunch stand. The place has been booming ever since, so much so that Sol's son moved to larger quarters in 2002. The new complex includes the MarketPlace, with more than 100 indoor shops and as many as 800 outdoor vendors; the Hartville Kitchen restaurant, bakery, and candy shop; Hartville Collectibles & Gifts; and Hartville Hardware & Lumber. More than a million shoppers visit the 12-acre complex each year. Special holiday and themed events are held throughout the year, and bus tours are especially welcome. The complex is open on Mondays, Thursdays, Fridays, and Saturdays. The outdoor flea market happens Mondays, Fridays, and Saturdays.

## 101 HOCKING HILLS

### 101A Hocking Hills Regional Welcome Center

**13178 State Route 664 South, Logan, OH 43138; 740-385-9706 or 800-hocking (462-5464)**

### 101B Hocking Hills Regional Welcome Center

**16197 Pike Street, Laurelville, OH 43135; 740-332-0516**
**hockinghills.com**
**explorehockinghills.com**

If you've never been to the Hocking Hills, stop at a visitor center to pick up maps and information on tours of the area by vehicle, horseback, or even hot-air balloon. Then take a look at the attractions. Hiking is a popular pastime in the area's state forests, parks, and preserves. There are also zipline, canopy, and climbing/rappelling tours, as well as biking, canoeing and kayaking, fishing, and golf. Indoors you can visit wineries, arts centers and galleries, museums, an opera house, and many unique shops. At the Hocking Hills Candleworks in Logan, for instance, you can mix and match scents to have a personally scented soy candle made just for you. Restaurants also abound. I can recommend Lake Hope State Park Lodge for a great meal with a fabulous view. If you decide to stay awhile, check out the Maple View Tree House from Among the Trees Lodging in Logan or the Buckeye Box cabin in McArthur.

## 102 JUNGLE JIM'S INTERNATIONAL MARKETS

**102A 4450 Eastgate South Drive, Cincinnati, OH 45245; 513-674-6000**
**102B 5440 Dixie Highway, Fairfield, OH 45014; 513-674-6000**
**junglejims.com**

These are grocery stores, but they're amazing ones. It boggles the mind. First, the food—there's more of everything than you can imagine. Just the cheese bar will leave you gasping. There are always food-sample stations, so take time to taste some seafood or fresh fruit. Don't miss my favorite spot, the coffee bar, with 50 varieties of coffee and 20 kinds of loose-leaf tea. Then there's the sightseeing. Examine a Navy fire truck, listen to the Cereal Bowl Band, use an outhouse photo booth, look for the scarecrow, the olive bar, the humidor, and, of course, Elvis. The stores offer tours, cooking classes, and Junglefest events like wine and beer festivals, barbecues, a Fall Smash, a Big Cheese Festival, murder mysteries, and the Weekend of Fire celebrating fiery foods, sauces, and marinades.

## 103 KINGS ISLAND

**6300 Kings Island Drive, Kings Island, OH 45034; 513-754-5700**
**visitkingsisland.com**

This massive amusement park comes with more than just roller coasters and thrill rides. It also includes Soak City—a water park with activities like the Zoom Flume, the Mondo Monsoon, and the Tropical Twister. There's also Dinosaurs Alive! with controllable animatronic dinosaurs, several races, and an Ultimate Stunt Show. At Camp Snoopy, a new extension of the Planet Snoopy kids' area, children are welcomed by members of the Peanuts Gang to lead Camptivities. Kids and parents can have double fun on Camp Snoopy's Soap Box Racers roller coaster, which runs forward, then backward. With a VIP ticket, you get front-of-the-line access to rides, behind-the-scenes tours, and reserved seating for shows. There are dozens of places to eat and drink, and all-day or all-season dining plans are available. There's also a pet resort on-site. Adjacent to the park is Great Wolf Lodge, with its own indoor water park.

## 104 LAKE METROPARKS FARMPARK

**8800 Euclid Chardon Road,**
**Kirtland, OH 44094**
**440-256-2122 or 800-366-3276**
**advkeen.co/farmpark**

The folks at Farmpark strive to help visitors connect to and understand the importance of their agricultural heritage. In addition to families, the park welcomes more than 100,000 students yearly from local schools.

Besides farm animals, crops, and gardens, their 235 acres include a plant science center and exhibits of farm machinery, plus a playground. Wagons drawn by horses or tractors are available to take visitors to different activities and are handicap-accessible. Daily activities include milking, by hand or by machine, and interacting with other farm animals. You'll also learn how the animals are bred and how they are used on a farm. Border collies put on daily herding demonstrations in Shepherd's Field. In the horse barn you can learn about grooming, harnessing, and driving horses. An afternoon wool demonstration can teach you everything you've always wanted to know about how raw wool gets from the sheep or alpaca to a sweater. At the plant science center there are daily demonstrations on beekeeping, honey harvesting, and hydroponics. Monthly events follow the seasons with an Ice Festival, Maple Sugaring weekends, Fall Harvest weekends, and more.

Visitors are welcome to bring their own picnics, or drinks and snacks are available in the gift shop.

## 105 THE OLIVE SCENE

**105A** **100 North Main Street,**
**Suite 145, Chagrin Falls, OH 44022**
**440-247-7999**
**105B** **19132 Old Detroit Road,**
**Rocky River, OH 44116**
**440-895-9999**
**105C** **5512 Liberty Avenue,**
**Vermilion, OH 44089**
**440-963-0504**
**theolivescene.com**

I visited the Vermilion store with friends who had been there before. They were enthusiastic and fearless about tasting infused oils, gourmet oils, robusto oils, and artisanal balsamic vinegars. There are also oils made from nuts and seeds. I was hesitant about the whole thing and never even mustered the courage to taste the aged vinegars. If you're a foodie, though, with an appreciation for textures and flavors that burst over your tongue, this is a day trip you have to take. The stores also sell table accessories, salts and seasonings, and gift sets. The owners of The Olive Scene make regular community appearances at festivals and farmer's markets. The three stores also offer private parties that include more than 50 tastings, with hors d'oeuvres and desserts.

## 106 RICHLAND CARROUSEL PARK

**75 North Main Street,**
**Mansfield, OH 44902**
**419-522-4223**
**richlandcarrousel.com**

It's such a charming, welcome surprise to drive into Mansfield and see a full-size carrousel spinning merrily under an airy pavilion. What could be more fun? It's bargain fun at that, since rides are only $1, or six for $5. As the Stinson Band Organ plays, you can choose from 30 horses or 22 menagerie figures that range from rabbits to ostriches to a lion and a tiger. The carrousel is handicap-accessible and can accommodate wheelchairs. If you want a fast ride, the outer ring travels at 6.77 mph. The inside ring travels at a more sedate pace, 3.71 mph. Don't forget to look up at the scenery panels in the center of the carousel, depicting scenes and people from Ohio. There is a snack bar available, and box lunches can be arranged as well. Groups, whether large or small, are welcome for parties, and there are Friday cookouts periodically. The park opened in 1991 with its newly built, hand-carved carousel. Each figure was built by the Carousel Works in Mansfield, which is sadly out of business, but a former employee is still carving rides at his shop, All Around Carousels. Large groups are welcome at the park, and private parties can be booked after 6 p.m. For First Fridays, the Carousel Café offers snacks and beverages.

## 107 ROGERS COMMUNITY FLEA MARKET & AUCTIONS

**45625 State Route 154,**
**Rogers, OH 44455**
**330-227-3233**
**Alternate Address:**
**45625 Walnut Street,**
**Rogers, OH 44455**
**rogersohio.com**

If it's Friday (or a first summer Saturday of the month), head to Rogers in northeast Ohio for the Sale. Cars start backing up at the lone red light in Rogers before 9 a.m. The flea market is open year-round; in the busy summer season, more than a 1,000 vendors can fill indoor and outdoor booths to accommodate shoppers who come from miles around. The Sale opens around 7:30 a.m. and stays open until the last vendor leaves. Indoor sellers tend to concentrate on a single product, like books, cheese, doughnuts (free samples!), health-and-beauty items, tools, or tires. Outdoor vendors sell wild conglomerations of goods that draw you in to look, try, haggle, and buy. There are plenty of food vendors on-site, plus a full restaurant. In-person and online auctions for everything from eggs to household goods to firewood and tractors happen at varying times during the month. An annual Spring Fling benefits Shriners Hospitals for Children.

## 108 SPRINGFIELD ANTIQUE SHOW & FLEA MARKET

**4401 South Charleston Pike,**
**Springfield, OH 45502**
**937-325-0053**
**advkeen.co/springfield_antique**

More than 20,000 shoppers visit the Springfield show for nine weekends every year. Most of the events are on Saturdays and Sundays, but two expanded Extravaganzas run Friday through Sunday.

Dozens of vendors are on hand for each event, plus a frozen-cocktail stand and a beer tent.

The events take place on the Clark County Fairgrounds, which has a handy campground for shoppers. Electric scooters are available for rent, and porters who work for tips can transport large items to your vehicle. There are graduated admission fees to enter the grounds.

## 109 TOLEDO ZOO & AQUARIUM

**2 Hippo Way, Toledo, OH 43609**
**419-385-5721**
**toledozoo.org**

Like all zoos of a certain age—this one is more than 100 years old—the Toledo Zoo has changed a lot. Where there used to be animals in cages, now there's a Tembo Trail complex, which provides 9,000 square feet of indoor space and 40,000 square feet of outdoor space, including a Hippoquarium. The zoo hasn't abandoned all its history, though. Many WPA buildings erected during the Depression are still in use, including the aquarium, built of stone and red brick and featuring porthole windows. Don't miss the gardens, fronted by a spectacular glass conservatory. Tours and classes are also part of the experience there. Many head to the Aerial Adventure Course to traverse 750 feet of aerial bridges and zipline over the Africa! exhibit. The course also includes the Quick Jump (30 feet), Flight Line (an 80-foot plunge) and a Challenge Course, with rope bridges, swinging log crossings, and horizontal climbing walls, among other obstacles.

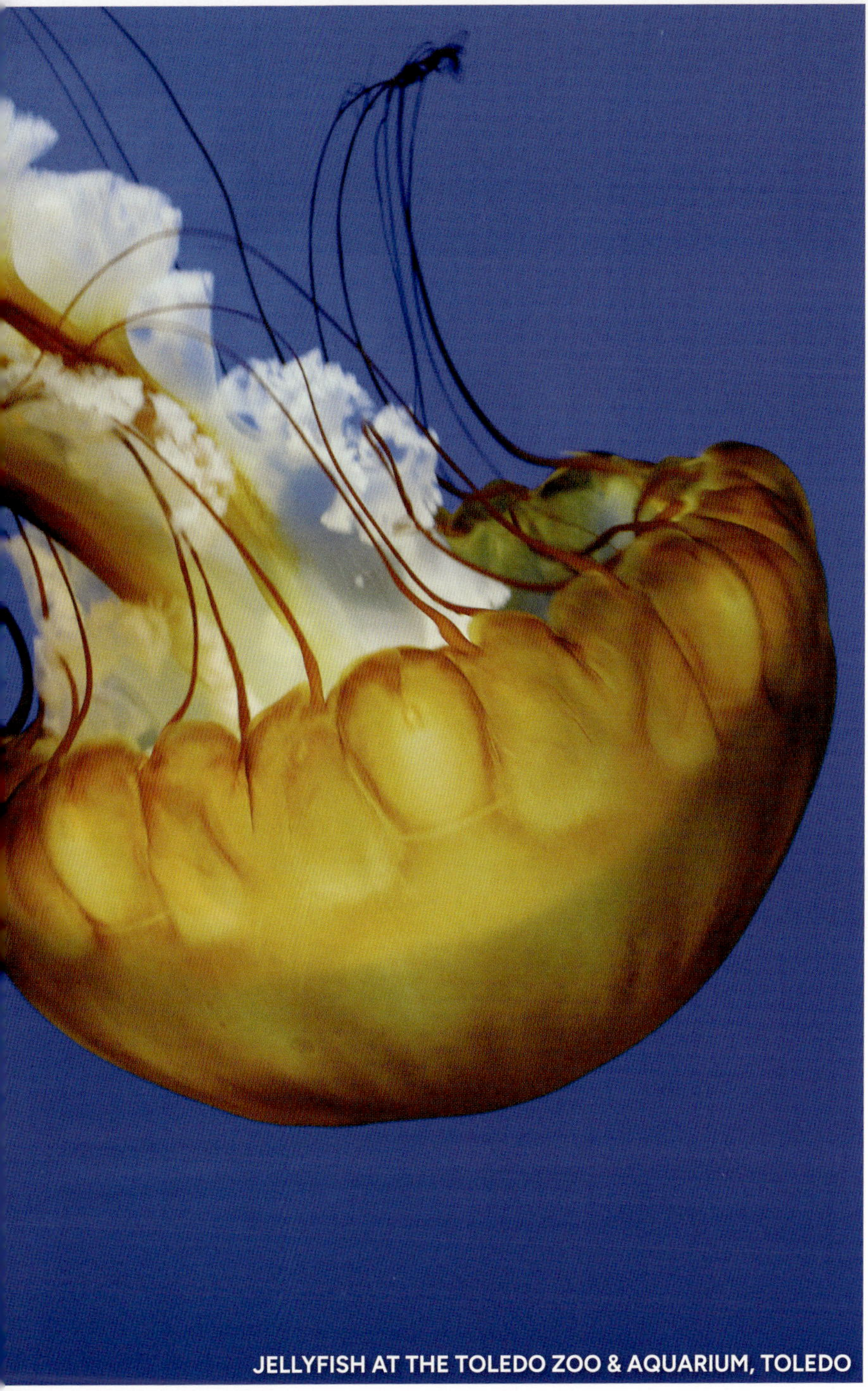

JELLYFISH AT THE TOLEDO ZOO & AQUARIUM, TOLEDO

CHINESE CULTURAL GARDEN, CLEVELAND

**Time and space for peaceful or prayerful contemplation are hallmarks of a public garden or arboretum.**

Yoga and tai chi are popular offerings, as are Japanese-style gardens. Some gardens listed here are for more-active people and include children's activities, play spaces, or hiking/biking trails.

## Welcome to
# GARDENS, FLOWERS & ARBORETUMS

**Holden Forests and Gardens is a merging of Holden Arboretum and Cleveland Botanical Garden and is the 12th largest public garden in the country. The organization "connects people with the wonder, beauty, and value of trees and plants" through research, education, and conservation.**



**Columbus**

Who doesn't love a topiary? At this park there are topiaries on lawns, topiaries in the water, topiaries in groupings, and topiaries in progress.



**Dayton**

A Children's Discovery Garden is a kid-friendly place with a Music Maze, raised sandboxes, a Fossil Cave, and a wading stream.

FAIRY DOORS AT HOLDEN ARBORETUM, KIRTLAND

## *Find out more about* GARDENS, FLOWERS & ARBORETUMS

### 110 COX ARBORETUM

**6733 North Springboro Pike, Dayton, OH 45449; 937-275-7275**
**metroparks.org/places-to-go/cox-arboretum**

Part of the Five Rivers Metroparks system, Cox is the home of the Tree Tower, which is so pretty you can't help but climb it, not even minding the 81 steps. A viewing platform at the top provides a panoramic view of the Miami Valley and the arboretum's conifer collection. In the 100-acre Ruth Cummings Mead Woodland, be sure to visit the two groves of pawpaw trees. The arboretum is also the home of the Bell Children's Maze, constructed of 1,175 boxwoods, and the Butterfly House. Wear a bright-yellow shirt to encourage butterfly landings. Pollinator Gardens are just outside the Butterfly House. The Conservation Corner and Zorniger Education Campus are used for education in sustainability, environmentalism, and restoration ecology.

### 111 DAWES ARBORETUM

**7770 Jacksontown Road, Newark, OH 43056; 740-323-2355 or 800-44-DAWES (32937)**
**dawesarb.org**

Nature lovers and self-taught naturalists Bertie and Beman Dawes planted more than 50,000 trees on their 293-acre farm before they founded the arboretum in 1929. Today, visitors come in every season to explore. The Japanese Garden is an especially exquisite, serene space, with flowing water that showcases the natural landscape. Don't miss Azalea Glen and the Cypress Swamp, home to many salamanders. You'll need good shoes and a permit to hike the woodland trails at Arboretum East. The Dutch Fork Wetlands feature an observation deck, six pools, and diverse wildlife. The Italianate Daweswood House Museum is also open for tours. On-site learning is a priority here and includes programs for children; learning resources for teachers; and lectures, tours, and pop-up exhibits for adults.

### 112 FELLOWS RIVERSIDE GARDENS

**123 McKinley Avenue, Youngstown, OH 44509; 330-740-7116**
**advkeen.co/fellows_gardens**

The 12-acre garden is part of the Mill Creek Metroparks in Youngstown. Since 1963, they've featured formal rose gardens, where new varieties are tested, as well as tree collections and displays of annuals and perennials. At the education center, a café and classrooms host lectures on horticulture and art. A Victorian gazebo and the Kidston Pavilion are frequently used for weddings, as well as photo backdrops. The garden's most colorful feature is provided by more than 40,000 spring bulbs, followed by seasonal displays of annuals and perennials. Garden tours and courses are available, and the Garden Café offers a good lunch selection. Yoga, tai chi, kids' clubs, and family-fun programs are also on the schedule.

POND WITH LILIES AT KINGWOOD CENTER GARDENS, MANSFIELD

## 113 HOLDEN FORESTS & GARDENS

**9550 Sperry Road,
Kirtland, OH 44094; 440-946-4400
holdenarb.org**

Trails wind through the gardens at Holden Arboretum, ranging from 0.75- mile to almost 3 miles long. They provide views of Corning Lake, conifer and beech-maple forests, and meadows filled with field-nesting birds. Be aware that some have steep steps. There are also two rhododendron gardens and a butterfly garden. The display garden includes a hedge collection and a lilac collection. A lotus pond and a lily pond showcase water plants. Interesting spots to visit include Buckeye Bud's Adventure Playground, which has a kid-size zipline; the 120-foot Kalberer Emergent Tower; and the Murch Canopy Walk, suspended 65 feet above the ground. One of the best features here, especially in winter, is the guided tour of Stebbins Gulch, a deep ravine microclimate.

## 114 KINGWOOD CENTER GARDENS

**50 North Trimble Road,
Mansfield, OH 44906; 419-522-0211
kingwoodcenter.org**

Formerly a private estate, Kingwood was opened to the public in 1953. Offices and a horticultural library are housed in Kingwood Hall. Scheduled guided tours are available. The hall is surrounded by 47 acres laid out in a variety of themes. There are seasonal and historic gardens; those dedicated to herbs; as well as terrace, woodland, and perennial gardens. The Allée between the hall and Draffan Fountain is an excellent spot from which to view spring flowers and flowering trees and shrubs. Admire the resident peacocks as you explore the grounds. Kingwood offers workshops, children's programming, and special events, and it is a popular wedding venue. Access to the B&O Bike Trail is near the Garden Gateway entrance.

## 115 SCHEDEL ARBORETUM & GARDENS

**19255 West Portage River South Road,
Elmore, OH 43416
419-862-3182 (use extension 1001
to arrange guided tours)
schedel-gardens.org**

The Schedel Foundation administers this 17-acre gem in accordance with the wishes of Marie and Joe Schedel, who spent years building their sanctuary. Visitors can sign up for a tour or meander on their own, discovering 25 different sculptures and multiple themed gardens. There are garden areas for roses, perennials, peonies, irises, tropical plants, a bonsai collection, a Japanese-inspired garden, and even a vegetable garden.

The Brown Center holds the McAlear Gallery, which hosts exhibits of unique artists from around the world, and a café on the Overlook Deck offers hors d'oeuvres, ice cream, and drinks. The Trellis Gallery and the Shack also hold collections and exhibits.

The Blair Museum of Lithophanes is now located in the Schedels' 1887 Victorian manor house after being moved from the Toledo Botanical Gardens in 2021. A lithophane, visitors discover, is a tiny porcelain plaque carved in three dimensions. When backlighted, the bare carving is transformed into an amazingly detailed scene.

The gardens are a popular wedding and event venue, and kids' camps are offered in summer.

## 116 SPRING GROVE CEMETERY & ARBORETUM

**4521 Spring Grove Avenue,**
**Cincinnati, OH 45232; 513-681-7526**
**springgrove.org**

It seems odd that an 1844 cemetery also calls itself an arboretum, but it was founded by members of the Cincinnati Men's Horticulture Society and later enhanced by a landscape architect who designed a "garden cemetery." More than 200 exotic trees were planted in the mid-1800s, though a small forest preserve in a ravine has remained untouched. In the 1920s, the flower collection was enlarged, and the arboretum continues to evolve today. The property is a National Historic Landmark and contains many State Champion trees, both native and non-native. Notables buried there include several Civil War generals; Supreme Court jurist Salmon P. Chase; prominent members of the Taft family; and business leaders like Bernard Kroger, William Procter, James Gamble, and Charles L. Fleischmann.

## 117 TOLEDO BOTANICAL GARDEN

**5403 Elmer Drive, Toledo, OH 43615**
**419-407-9700**
**metroparkstoledo.com/explore-your-parks/toledo-botanical-garden-metropark**

The Toledo Botanical Garden's Discovery Trail encompasses all 66 acres of the garden, which includes the award-winning Daylily Walk. Themed spaces include an inclusive garden, an herb garden, a shade garden, a vegetable garden, a rose garden, a perennial garden, and a pioneer garden. There are also a dozen sculptures. An artists' village includes buildings for potters, glassblowers, stained glass artists, and more. A summer jazz concert series fills the garden with music. The garden is also host to the annual Crosby Festival of the Arts.

## 118 TOPIARY PARK

**480 East Town Street,**
**Columbus, OH 43215; 614-645-0197**
**GPS: 39.9611°, -82.9876°**

Topiaries are living sculptures fashioned out of plants, and one of the fascinating things here is that you can see a topiary in the making. On some of the living yew sculptures, metal skeletons can still be seen as a ghost image of the eventual fully grown topiary. The garden's centerpiece is a topiary re-creation of Georges Seurat's painting, *A Sunday Afternoon on the Isle of La Grande Jatte.* The scene includes 54 human figures, 8 boats, 3 dogs, a monkey, and a cat. You have to stand in a particular spot to see it from the right viewpoint, but if you know the painting, the view is unmistakable. The 7-acre park, which was once the site of the Ohio School for the Deaf, also showcases 220 trees in 25 varieties, formal flowerbeds, and walking trails.

## 119 WEGERZYN GARDENS METROPARK

**1301 East Siebenthaler Avenue,**
**Dayton, OH 45414; 937-275-7275**
**advkeen.co/wegerzyn_gardens**

This is a good place for your kids to get dirty and wet. The Children's Discovery Garden encourages hands-on activity. Kids are encouraged to touch the plants, play in the dirt, experiment with sand art, and splash in the water. The Discovery Garden is open March through December, though the park itself is open all year. For adults, the formal Federal, English, and Victorian gardens (and the rose garden) attract home gardeners looking for design ideas and techniques. The Stillwater River Trail is the place to be for spring color and autumn leaves, and it provides access to other Metroparks. The whole family can search for fairy shrimp in the vernal pools of the Swamp Forest or hike the 1-mile Marie Aull Nature Trail. While you're there, look for the Pedestal Oak between the parking lot and gate.

WEGERZYN GARDENS METROPARK, DAYTON

**Day-trippers in Ohio expect to find wineries along the shores of Lake Erie and the Ohio River, but there are actually distinct wine regions across the state.**

The Appalachian region, Canal Country, Capital City region, Lake Erie Shores and Islands, and the Ohio River Valley are all key growing areas.

*Welcome to*

# GOOD SPIRITS & GOOD TIMES



**Youngstown**

There's a definite motorcycle theme running through the brews here, and why not? Biker Brewhouse is located inside a Harley Davidson dealership.



**Berea and Madison**

Advertising itself as family-friendly, Cornerstone was founded to offer an alternative for northeast Ohio beer drinkers.



**Cortland**

This winery started out in a warehouse, but the owners were always on the lookout for a better winery ambience. They've found a "just like home" atmosphere here.



**Cincinnati**

Fibonacci calls itself a nanobrewery, with four foundational beers plus seasonals. But what is it with the maple-bacon doughnuts?



**Akron**

The Grape and Granary Winery and Renaissance Artisan Distillers are housed at this homebrewing supply store, where you can also buy the materials for beer, sake, soda, mead, cheese, vinegar, and kombucha.



**Vandalia**

With a name like that, and daily Hoppy Hours, you just have to drop in, don't you? They even have an ugly mug club.



**Hartville**

Fall is a great time to visit Maize Valley. Fall harvest events include a corn maze; hot-air balloon launch; and an appearance by Megasaurus, a fire-breathing, car-crushing metal dinosaur.



**Cincinnati**

The oldest winery in the state, Meier's has produced wine since the 1800s, at one time growing grapes on North Bass Island.



**Bidwell**

This is a friendly place, meant for gatherings of all kinds. Bring a picnic lunch and the family dog (on a leash), and enjoy the day.

### 129 NORTHSIDE DISTILLING CO. ...................... 79

**Cincinnati**

Founded in a stereotypical little white barn, this distillery focuses on corn whiskey, moonshine, vodka, and bourbon.

### 130 OHIO WINE PRODUCERS ASSOCIATION ........................ 79

**Geneva-on-the-Lake**

For a comprehensive list of wineries by their region, plus information about wine trails and events, check out the Ohio Wine Association.

### 131 OLD FIREHOUSE WINERY ........... 80

**Geneva**

This winery really is an old fire-house. One of the founders, Don Woodward, is a retired fire-fighter, EMT, and a grand-son of a member of the original fire department.

### 132 SOINE VINEYARDS ............... 80

**Powell**

Winemaking is taken very seriously here at Soine. Their wines have won multiple awards.

### 133 STALEY MILL FARM & INDIAN CREEK DISTILLERY ............. 80

**New Carlisle**

A fifth-generation Staley carries on the family whiskey-making tradition on the 160-acre family farm.

### 134 URBAN PINE WINERY & EATERY .............. 80

**Maumee**

Stop in here to help winemakers craft any type of wine you want. You can even add your own custom labels.

### 135 WATERSHED DISTILLERY ...............................81

**Columbus**

The distillery produces bourbon, vodka, gin, and nocino, a black walnut liqueur. After a tour, visitors are welcome to visit the bar and restaurant.

NORTHSIDE DISTILLING CO., CINCINNATI

## *Find out more about*
## GOOD SPIRITS & GOOD TIMES

### 120 BIKER BREWHOUSE

**BikeTown Harley Davidson**
**5700 Patriot Boulevard, Unit B,**
**Youngstown, OH 44515**
**330-520-2266**
**bikerbrewhouse.net**

What are you in the mood for: High Octane Stout, EZ Rider Pilsner, or Cruisin' Christmas Ale? The drinks here are motorcycle-inspired, and all are brewed with fresh, local ingredients. High Octane Stout, for instance, is a combination of Biker Brewhouse's stout and the High Octane Coffee Company's cold-brewed South American coffee. Beer is available in sampler sizes, pints, growlers, or kegs. Appetizers and light food are also on the menu. For relaxing with a brew in biker ambience, there's a pub table in the dealership's lounge, plus a brewhouse and balcony upstairs. An outdoor patio welcomes four-legged friends, and a meeting room is available for private parties.

### 121 CORNERSTONE BREWING COMPANY

**58 Front Street, Berea, OH 44017**
**440-239-9820**
**facebook.com/cornerstoneberea**

Inventive and enticing names are a staple of brewpubs, and Cornerstone is no exception. At either location, try out Eirinn Rosanna, an Irish Red Ale, or Pleasurable Demise, an apricot-flavored IPA. If you're feeling adventurous, you might want to go for an Erie Blü, which is actually rose-colored. The brewers promise a "fruity beerie kick" from the 6 pounds of raspberries and blackberries that go into every barrel. A full menu is available to go along with tastings. Start with brewers' pretzels, move on to beer cheese soup, and complete your meal with fish or chicken diablo.

### 122 COUNTRY PORCH WINERY

**2282 Wilson Sharpsville Road**
**(State Route 305), Cortland, OH 44410**
**330-638-0000**
**countryporchwinery.com**

A very pretty front porch with rocking chairs and a small bar welcomes visitors to this winery. Using locally sourced juices, the wines here are inventive and tasty. Country Café, for instance, is made with coffee. Seyval Certain Gold contains hints of pear, apple, and lemon. Celebrate D'Vine is a crisp apple meant to be served with holiday meals. The sweet wines include Off the Rocker, made with raspberries, and a summery blend called Peachy Summer Passion. The semi-sweets feature an interesting Stone Cellar merlot and an Italian-style Pinot Grigio called Daisy for Me. On the drier side, guests can enjoy Scenic Route, a Noiret with the flavors of cherries, pepper, black raspberry, blueberry, and plum.

The winery offers a fresh seasonal menu with a variety of appetizers, soups, and homemade flatbread sandwiches and pizzas. The Country Porch is open afternoons and evenings, Wednesdays through Saturdays.

## 123 FIBONACCI BREWING COMPANY

**1445 Compton Road, Cincinnati, OH 45231; 513-832-1422**
**fibbrew.com**

Yes, that's a mathematical reference in the name, but you'll have to ask them to explain it. Ninety percent of the brewery's products are sourced on-site and from local farms. Offerings include Tertiary, a rye strong ale; Calculus, a cream ale; and Chestnut Hypothesis, a golden ale. Seasonally, they also produce Lavender Lemonade Wine Punch and Mulled Wine.

Fibonacci's is a socially responsible, majority woman-owned operation. They host a Little Free Library and a monthly farmer's market with SNAP and Produce Perks. There is also a seed-swapping station in the brewery to aid local food insecurity. The brewery's calendar is filled with community events like book clubs and sewing circles. Food trucks come in regularly for the farmer's markets, plant swaps, game nights, and live music nights.

## 124 THE GRAPE & GRANARY

**915 Home Avenue, Akron, OH 44310**
**330-633-7223 or 800-695-9870**
**renartisan.com**

It started out as a simple homebrewing and winemaking supply store, until the owners decided to try their hands at winemaking and distilling themselves. The Grape and Granary Winery and Renaissance Artisan Distillers are now combined with the supply store. On the supply side, you can buy ingredients and equipment to make your own soda, wine, liquor, sake, cheese, vinegar, and kombucha. The "Wine on Premise" program at the Granary allows shoppers to work with winemakers to produce their own customized wines. At the distillers, visitors can tour the operation and choose tastings from gin, single malt whiskey, grappa, rum, coffee liqueur, and (mmmmmm) limoncello.

## 125 THE HAIRLESS HARE BREWERY

**738 West National Road, Vandalia, OH 45377; 937-387-6476**
**hairlessharebrewery.com**

Matt Harris and Mike Legg, guys with a sense of humor, founded the brewery in 2013, and they seem to be doing well for themselves. They brew on-site, aiming both for craft beer aficionados and those new to the style. They offer British Hare ESB; Hairless Tang, which is a tangerine wheat; Luck of the Hare Irish stout; and something called Rye the Hell Knot. In 2019, the owners added craft ciders, including Strawberry Patch, Tropical Sunrise, and Blueberry Hill. There is also a limited menu of pizza, starters, wings, and sandwiches—perfect food to go with beer.

## 126 MAIZE VALLEY WINERY & BREWERY

**6193 Edison Street Northeast (State Route 619), Hartville, OH 44632**
**330-877-8344**
**maizevalley.com**

First there's the winery, where a variety of wines are made from Concord and French-American Hybrid grapes grown right on the farm's 10 acres. The offerings include Big Red Pecker Wine (named for a rooster), Apple Pie Wine with notes of cinnamon and brown sugar, and a sparkling White Winter Wine. Then there's the brewery. Among the beers available are Garnet Grenade, an imperial red IPA; Muck Monster imperial stout; and Lock, Stock, and Brandy Barrel, which is a malty stock ale aged in, of course, brandy barrels.. Along with your tastings, appetizers and desserts or casual lunches and dinners can be added. Then there's the Maize Valley Market, where produce grown on the farm is sold. Special events are a big deal at Maize Valley, and they're family friendly. Besides fall and holiday festivities, there are classic car shows; craft dinners; live music nights; and my personal favorite event, Mimosa Saturdays.

## 127 MEIER'S WINE CELLARS

**6955 Plainfield Road,**
**Cincinnati, OH 45236; 513-891-2900**
**meierswinecellars.com**

They're the oldest and largest wine producer in the state, thanks to grape juice. Meier's started out as a grape juice company in the late 1800s, then made wine, and then returned to its roots during Prohibition, making a sparkling Catawba juice. Today it still produces sparkling nonalcoholic grape juice, along with 45 varieties of wine. Its best-known product is #44 Cream Sherry, though I'm partial to the blackberry wine. When you visit, take advantage of the hors d'oeuvres available to complement tastings. The retail store and tasting room are open to the public, but check online for hours.

## 128 MERRY FAMILY WINERY & OLD MILL CRAFT BEER

**2376 State Route 850,**
**Bidwell, OH 45614; 740-245-9463**
**merryfamilywinery.com**

A surprise offering on the wine list is Mothman Legend, a mysterious dry red. You might have to be an Ohioan to understand that, as the "Mothman" is the subject of local lore. There's also a Southern Belle Muscato and a Sweet Granny apple wine. The Blue Merry Blush is a red grape/blueberry blend that I'm told, pairs well with a blueberry muffin. Bad Kitty Sangria is a blend of red grapes and citrus. Old Mill Craft beers, made with hops grown on-site, include wheat, pilsner, ale, IPA, and lager. Root beer and hard cider are also made here.

## 129 NORTHSIDE DISTILLING CO.

**922 Race Street,**
**Cincinnati, OH 45202; (513) 202-6532**
**northsidedistilling.com**

This Cincinnati distillery, the first to be located downtown since Prohibition, calls itself an honest, no-frills business. They're open for tours and tastings on Friday and Saturday evenings. Offerings include bourbon whiskey, gin, vodka, American Agave, and rum. Specialty spirits, which can be privately labeled, include moonshine, corn whiskey, and something called Stillhouse Chickow! The distillery also produces Braille Bourbon Whiskey in partnership with the Cincinnati Association for the Blind and Visually Impaired. A portion of the proceeds from the product goes to CABVI.

## 130 OHIO WINE PRODUCERS ASSOCIATION

**1 South Broadway, Geneva, OH 44041**
**440-466-4417 or 800-227-6972**
**ohiowines.org**

Suppose you'd like to explore some of the state's wineries but have no idea how to go about it. Head to the Ohio Wine Producers Association's website for collected information on Ohio's seven wine trails and the wineries by region. Each regional page includes a map, contact information, an address, and a brief description of each winery. Also included is information on nearby attractions, events, lodging, and even transportation options for those who imbibe too much. Festivals and events are also listed on the website.

## 131 OLD FIREHOUSE WINERY

**5499 Lake Road East,**
**Geneva-on-the-Lake, OH 44041**
**440-466-9300**
**oldfirehousewinery.com**

Its logo is, of course, a Dalmatian wearing a red fire helmet. Old Firehouse (housed in the village's first fire station) is a large, busy place in the resort town of Geneva-on-the-Lake, and fun-seeking day-trippers make it a priority stop. They don't even have to be wine drinkers. There's a vintage Ferris wheel at the edge of the lake; live music on summer weekends; and regular events like a craft fair, a Celtic Feis (festival), a barbecue fest, a clambake, and a blues festival. Then there's the wine. The Firehouse label includes regular offerings, like Concord, Catawba, and Niagara, but there's also Apple Ice wine and Big Eli dessert wine.

## 132 SOINE VINEYARDS

**3510 Clark Shaw Road,**
**Powell, OH 43065; 740-362-5741**
**soinevineyards.com**

Visitors are welcome to tour the winery and take advantage of the tasting room, but please note that Soine (soy-nee) isn't open every day. Call and check for hours. Wines offered include award winners such as Fusion, Landot Noir, Chambourcin, Cayuga White, and Traminette. Appetizers, pizza, and nonalcoholic drinks are available with tastings. Music is offered on summer weekends.

## 133 STALEY MILL FARM & INDIAN CREEK DISTILLERY

**7095 Staley Road,**
**New Carlisle, OH 45344**
**937-846-1443**
**staleymillfarmanddistillery.com**

From the 1860s until Prohibition, the Staley family made whiskey. Production didn't begin again until 2011, when the current member of the Staley family and her husband began again with a double copper distilling method. The family takes pride in crafting what they call "frontier whiskey" in small batches using traditional methods. Aged and unaged rye whiskey, bourbon mash whiskey, and gin are sold here, along with a farm-produced maple syrup that includes a bit of rye. The farm hosts musical events, movies, holiday open houses, living-history events, and even a sip-and-smoke day. The distillery is open Tuesdays through Saturdays, with Sunday hours at Christmastime. There's a rustic tasting bar and retail shop, and tours of the distillery and farm are offered.

## 134 URBAN PINE WINERY & EATERY

**3415 Briarfield Boulevard,**
**Maumee, OH 43537; 567-703-1281**
**urbanpinewinery.com**

This family-owned and female-operated business sources its grapes from around the world and pairs them with brunch, lunch, and dinner menus. Wines are also paired with some delectable desserts. With a cheesecake flight, for instance, try the Cascade Riesling. A molten caramel brownie deserves—what else?—chocolate raspberry port.

Their white wines include offerings like Anna, a German Gewurztraminer, and Paradise, a sweet Moscato. Among the reds are Nora Rose, an Italian cabernet, and Trek, a dark-purple Argentinian malbec. If sangrias are your favorite, you can't go wrong with cinnamon pomegranate.

The winery offers live music regularly and hosts special events throughout the year.

## 135 WATERSHED DISTILLERY

**1145 Chesapeake Avenue, Suite D, Columbus, OH 43212; 614-357-1936**
**watersheddistillery.com**

With careful attention to detail and a passion for their work, the partners at Watershed craft products the old-fashioned way, with deliberate thoughtfulness. They proudly offer tours of the distillery (they last more than an hour) and then invite participants to visit their bar and restaurant, open evenings, Tuesdays through Saturdays. Besides their own bourbon, vodka, gin, and nocino, the Watershed bar offers a full slate of wines and beers, plus non-alcoholic drinks. The restaurant's sophisticated menu includes dishes made with the distillery's own products.

**George Remus, known as "King of the Bootleggers," moved to Cincinnati during Prohibition and, at one point, owned roughly 35% of all liquor in America. He helped inspire the character of Jay Gatsby.**

OHIO STATE REFORMATORY, MANSFIELD

## There's something compelling about an authentic historic building.

Maybe it's the thought of walking in the footsteps of long-passed people. Though Ohio is home to structures that date back centuries (see Great Serpent Mound, page 119), its architectural history is relatively recent. Still, there's much here to appreciate.

## *Welcome to* HISTORIC BUILDINGS & ARCHITECTURE

**Ohio's flag is the only state flag that isn't rectangular.**

### 146 STAN HYWET HALL & GARDENS .......... 88

**Akron**

If you've ever fantasized about living with grace and elegance in a turn-of-the-twentieth-century mansion, this is the place to feed that fantasy.

### 147 THOMAS A. EDISON BIRTHPLACE .......... 88

**Milan**

Even a genius starts out tripping over his own baby feet. Get to know Edison at the home where he spent his early years.

### 148 ZOAR VILLAGE .......... 89

**Zoar**

The tiny hamlet of Zoar isn't just a collection of historic buildings, frozen in time. More than 100 people still live in the 18th-century homes.

*Find out more about*

# HISTORIC BUILDINGS & ARCHITECTURE

## 136 CINCINNATI UNION TERMINAL

**Cincinnati Museum Center,**
**1301 Western Avenue,**
**Cincinnati, OH 45203; 513-287-7000**
**cincymuseum.org/union-terminal**

The western hemisphere's largest half dome—106 feet high and 180 feet across—soars over the entry to this 1930s-era passenger rail station. The principal architects were Alfred T. Fellheimer and Steward Wagner, with Paul Philippe Cret and Roland Wank serving as design consultants. More than 18,000 square feet of artwork originally adorned the station, including 23 Winold Reiss mosaic murals depicting timelines for the United States and for Cincinnati. Decorator Pierre Bourdelle painted ceilings with fantasy murals and constructed wall murals of carved linoleum. Two Maxfield Keck bas-relief carvings are in the rotunda. Some of the art was removed when the terminal was converted into a center for museums.

## 137 CLEVELAND ARCADE

**401 Euclid Avenue,**
**Cleveland, OH 44114; 216-575-1234**
**theclevelandarcade.com**

This five-story Victorian-era atrium spans the space between two taller buildings on each side. Balconies on the taller buildings overlook the atrium. A skylight stretches for 300 feet and is 100 feet high. Built in 1890, the structure was first used as a shopping mall. It was the first building in Cleveland to be listed on the National Register of Historic Places. In recent years, there's been a revitalization. One building has been repurposed as a Hyatt Regency Hotel. Shops and restaurants have begun to populate the atrium and the other buildings again.

## 138 GERMAN VILLAGE

**German Village Meeting Haus,**
**588 South 3rd Street,**
**Columbus, OH 43215**
**(614) 221-6623 or 800-354-2657**
**germanvillage.com**

This meticulously preserved neighborhood near downtown Columbus was developed in the mid-1800s by German immigrants. They built redbrick homes and breweries and preserved their German culture and language. The area began to decline during Prohibition, and by the 1950s it had become a slum. Revitalization began with the organization of the German Village Society and the German Village Commission. Strict zoning keeps the village mostly residential, with a limited commercial area. Walking carefully along the humped brick sidewalks, visitors can enjoy peeking at the tiny front gardens behind wrought iron fences and the tidy German-style homes. A favorite spot for many day-trippers is the Book Loft (see page 38), which spreads through several attached buildings on 3rd Street.

## 139 HALE FARM & VILLAGE

**2686 Oak Hill Road, Bath, OH 44210**
**330-666-3711**
**advkeen.co/hale_farm**

Administered by the Western Reserve Historical Society, this living-history village preserves the story of the Western Reserve, which was ceded from Connecticut and opened for settlement in the late 1700s. Visitors are invited to participate in the immersive culture at Hale. Costumed docents guide visitors and help them learn about farming, crafts and trades, and colonial history. There are regular lectures and programs for adults; children can partake in farm chores and historic crafts and trades, and attend programs ranging from maple sugaring to following the Underground Railroad. The public is also welcome to reserve space in the village for weddings and special events. (See also Made in Ohio Arts and Crafts Festival, page 54)

## 140 KIRTLAND TEMPLE

**7809 Joseph Street,**
**Kirtland, OH 44094; 440-256-1830**
**kirtlandtemple.org**

The 1833 temple was the first to be built by the Church of Jesus Christ of Latter-Day Saints. The building was constructed of local Berea Sandstone in a mix of Federal, Greek Revival, and Gothic Revival styles. Joseph Smith, the church's founder, said several miracles, including a vision of the celestial kingdom, occurred in the temple. Visitors are offered a general one-hour tour, group tours, or special tours, including a Streets of the Saints Tour and a Cemetery Tour. For the Basement to Bell Tower Tour, the recommendations are flexibility and clothes that you're OK with getting a bit dirty. There's also a Handyman Tour, which costs $10 and is perfect for those with a sense of humor. A Spiritual Formation Center offers group and personal spiritual retreats.

## 141 MALABAR FARM STATE PARK

**4050 Bromfield Road, Lucas, OH 44843; 419-892-2784**
**malabarfarm.org**

Pulitzer Prize–winning author Louis Bromfield built the Big House at Malabar Farm in 1940 after serving in WW I and living in France and India. Some of his novels and screenplays became movies, and he moved in Hollywood circles. On a tour of the Big House, you'll see the room where Humphrey Bogart and Lauren Bacall spent part of their honeymoon. Pugh Cabin, a day-use rental facility in the park, is part of the Shawshank Trail, since a scene from the movie *The Shawshank Redemption* was filmed there. The state park also includes a restaurant, a 19-bed hostel, and primitive camping. On the tractor-drawn farm wagon tour, you'll learn about farm techniques Bromfield used, like maple sugaring, no-till farming, strip cropping, contour farming, and grazing cells. Many locations on the tour are part of Bromfield's nonfiction work *Pleasant Valley*.

## 142 PAUL LAURENCE DUNBAR HOUSE

**219 North Paul Laurence Dunbar Street, Dayton, OH 45402; 937-224-7061**
**advkeen.co/dunbar_house**

Dunbar was one of the first African Americans to support himself entirely by writing. He was a renowned poet and author, producing a dozen books of poetry and four novels. He also wrote short stories and popular song lyrics. Admission is free, and the carefully preserved home is open Friday through Sunday. A visitor center is around the corner on Edison Street, where a film and more exhibits and artifacts are available.

## 143 ROSCOE VILLAGE

**600 North Whitewoman Street, Coshocton, OH 43812**
**740-622-7644 or 800-877-1830**
**roscoevillage.com**

This day trip will be a little slower than most, aboard the restored *Monticello III,* a horse-powered canal boat that transports visitors along part of the historic Ohio and Erie Canal at Roscoe Village, near Coshocton. The canal was a thriving concern from 1830 until the advent of railroads in 1861, and it continued to move local goods until the flood of 1913. In the late 1960s, Roscoe Village's revival began with the restoration of the 1840 tollhouse. Today, along with the authentic canal boat, visitors can take living-history tours through period homes and businesses, enjoy the gardens, and see a film about the canal era. Shops and restaurants are also available. The Johnson-Humrickhouse Museum located in the village has permanent exhibits on Native American and Early American history. (See also Ohio Canal System, page 135)

## 144 SAUDER VILLAGE

**22611 State Route 2, Archbold, OH 43502; 800-590-9755**
**saudervillage.org**

Take a train or buggy ride to begin your exploration at Sauder, which spreads over more than 200 acres. Some 40 historic buildings are collected here, including a farm shop originally used by the founder, woodworker Erie Sauder. There's also a cabinet shop, barbershop, medical office, school, water-powered gristmill, the Elmira Train Depot, and St. Mark's Lutheran Church. Costumed docents are available in homesteads and farm buildings. Visitors can watch blacksmiths, glassblowers, bakers, spinners, and farmers work as they did in pioneer times. Special events, like apple butter weekends, rug-hooking classes, a farmer's market, and Harry Potter Day go on all year long. The village includes the Doughbox Bakery and the Barn Restaurant, plus a café, ice-cream parlor, and coffee shop. You can even stay on the grounds, at the Sauder Heritage Inn or the Sauder Village Campground.

## 145 SCHOENBRUNN VILLAGE

**1984 East High Avenue,
New Philadelphia, OH 44663
330-808-4815 or 800-686-6124
advkeen.co/schoenbrunn
advkeen.co/schoenbrunn_village**

The Ohio country was still largely a wilderness in 1772, and few Europeans had visited the area. This restored village takes you back to those days, when Rev. David Zeisberger led 28 Moravians to the Tuscarawas Valley to serve as missionaries to the Delaware Indians. Their settlement lasted only five years, but another Moravian minister from nearby Dover later led an effort to salvage the village. Today, Historic Schoenbrunn consists of 16 reconstructed log buildings, a church, and the original cemetery. Costumed docents tell the story of a unique blending of German and Native American cultures. The visitor center offers an introductory film. *Trumpet in the Land,* a nearby outdoor drama (page 15), tells the story of Zeisberger's mission.

## 146 STAN HYWET HALL & GARDENS

**714 North Portage Path,
Akron, OH 44303; 330-836-5533
stanhywet.org**

This lovely estate was the home of the Seiberling family, founders of the Goodyear Tire and Rubber Company. It was completed in 1915 and named *Stan Hywet,* Old English for "stone quarry." The 68-room Tudor Revival house is surrounded by lagoons, terraces, formal gardens, and greenhouses. It's been named the #1 house tour in America, and rightly so. You can lose yourself here. Imagine being served breakfast in the four-poster curtained bed of the master bedroom. Climb the tower to watch sunshine play across the stained-glass windows. Admire the fanciful wallpaper in the nursery, or pretend the Round Room is your private hideaway. The Seiberlings always intended Stan Hywet to be a vibrant part of its community, so today the estate and its gardens are popular destinations.

## 147 THOMAS A. EDISON BIRTHPLACE

**9 North Edison Drive,
Milan, OH 44846; 419-499-2135
tomedison.org**

It's fascinating to walk through the childhood home of a genius and wonder about his formative years. Did he look at candlelight and think, "There has to be a better way?" Maybe. It's fun to think about, anyway. Thomas Edison was born here in 1847, lived in the home until he was 7, then purchased it himself in 1906, surprised to find the rooms still lit by candles. After his death in 1931, Edison's widow and daughter decided to use the house as a memorial to his remarkable life. It was opened as a museum on the centennial of his birth. His descendants still serve on the board of trustees, with a great-great-great-nephew as president. Exhibits include family mementos and documents, plus examples of some of his early inventions.

THE HISTORIC ZOAR VILLAGE, ZOAR

## 148 ZOAR VILLAGE

**Zoar Store & Visitor's Center, 198 Main Street, Zoar, OH 44697**
**330-874-3011 or 800-262-6195**
**historiczoarvillage.com**

German Separatists founded Zoar more than 200 years ago, in 1817. They considered it a utopia—a "sanctuary from evil." For more than 80 years, it was a thriving communal settlement. The religious community disbanded after the death of its founder, Joseph Bimeler, and the property was divided among the remaining residents. Today, the Zoar Community Association and the Ohio History Connection maintain a dozen of the historic homes as living-history museums. A formal 3-acre flower garden in Zoar is based on the Book of Revelation and includes a central Tree of Life representing Christ. Holiday and seasonal events, including a spring Maifest, are held each year, and there are school programs, classes, and lectures. Visitors can tour the museums and gardens, stroll through the village, learn to weave a rug, or forge a nail. History talks are held on the first Saturday of each month. You may also want to walk the quaint streets of the tiny town of Zoar that encompasses the village.

**For a Midwestern state, Ohio boasts some beautiful islands, complete with scenic vistas and nightlife with a definite island vibe.**

Kelleys Island is a bit of an upscale place, with pricey (but so worth it) bed-and-breakfast inns. South Bass Island, with the feisty tourist town of Put-in-Bay, is where that nightlife can be found. Tiny Middle Bass Island is known for its winery history and its more-modest lifestyle. North Bass has no commercial development and just a few dozen residents.

# Welcome to ISLAND DESTINATIONS

SUNSET FROM THE SHORES OF KELLEYS ISLAND

## *Find out more about* ISLAND DESTINATIONS

### 149 KELLEYS ISLAND

**240 East Lakeshore Drive,**
**Kelleys Island, OH 43438**
**419-746-2360**
**kelleysislandchamber.com**

This is one of the most popular day trips in northern Ohio. From Sandusky, Port Clinton, or Marblehead, hop on a ferry with your bicycle and a picnic basket, and spend the day in an island state of mind. Don't worry: if you're not a cyclist, there are plenty of golf carts for rent (be sure to ask if the battery is fully charged). The downtown area is filled with graceful Victorian homes and bed-and-breakfasts. The three-story Kelleys Mansion is open for tours, and it even has a widow's walk (a raised platform harking back to the days when sailing widowed many women). Near the mansion, don't miss Inscription Rock, carved with Native American symbols. Have lunch, explore the town, see the state park, and enjoy your day.

### 150 MIDDLE BASS ISLAND

**Middle Bass, OH 43446**
**866-644-6727**
**middlebass.org**

Middle Bass was home to the Lonz, Bretz, and Rehberg wineries, and long rows of grapes once dominated the island. Today, the Lonz property has been incorporated into Middle Bass Island State Park. Surprisingly, the island boasts some Civil War history. Confederates disguised as passengers from Canada boarded the lake steamer *Philo Parsons* and sailed it to Middle Bass, where they attacked and sank the *Island Queen*. Their ultimate objective was the USS *Michigan*, but they were foiled. Returning to Canada, most of the raiders were captured and one was hanged. Besides the state park and its campground, the island has several restaurants, golf cart rentals, a general store, four nature preserves, and plenty of birding opportunities.

### 151 NORTH BASS ISLAND

**Isle St. George, OH 43436**
**419-734-4424**
**ohiodnr.gov/go-and-do/plan-a-visit/find-a-property/north-bass-island-state-park**

There is no scheduled ferry service to this island, so access is by private boat or plane. Only a few families live here, and children must go to school off-island. Firelands Winery in Sandusky leases land from the state park for a vineyard, thus maintaining the island's heritage. Otherwise, there is no commercial development. At the state park, which occupies most of the 688-acre island, primitive camping is available by special permit. Boat tie-up is free, and fishing requires only an Ohio license.

### 152 SOUTH BASS ISLAND

**Put-in-Bay, OH 43456**
**419-285-2832**
**visitputinbay.com**

Shaped like a lopsided barbell, South Bass has a small northern section that is mostly residential, an isthmus that is home to the 352-foot-tall Perry's Victory and International Peace Memorial, and a larger southern section that holds the tourist town of Put-in-Bay. There you can hop the Tour Train (powered by Jeep) to see the sights, but be aware that pickup service at each stop can be erratic. Be sure to visit the Peace Memorial, which commemorates the Battle of Lake Erie during the War of 1812. Commander Oliver Hazard Perry sailed from Put-in-Bay to defeat the British, and after doing so, famously reported, "We have met the enemy, and they are ours." After your tour, retire to a bar or restaurant in town to enjoy some live music, a cool drink, and the Key West–like ambience.

**Ohio is home to 77 named islands. The largest is Kelleys Island, which is roughly 4.3 square miles and has a year-round population of about 300 people.**

TOLEDO HARBOR LIGHTHOUSE

**Given their purpose and history, lighthouses automatically evoke feelings of romance and adventure.**

You want to know their stories, how they were built, the people who served in them, and what happened to them after their era was over. You'll be happy to know that some of these lighthouses are still open to the public as museums or attractions. Even those that are closed to the public are still frequently visited and photographed.

*Welcome to*

# LIGHTHOUSES

**The lighthouses in Ohio play an essential safety role for the state's nine commercial ports along Lake Erie, including the Port of Cleveland, which ships directly to Europe.**



**Marblehead**

First opened in 1820, this is the oldest lighthouse in continuous operation on the United States' side of the Great Lakes. It was also home to the first female lighthouse keeper in the United States.



**Port Clinton**

This sturdy-looking structure was restored in 2014 before it was moved to a new waterfront home in August 2016.



**Put-in-Bay**

A research and academic team from The Ohio State University hosts tours of this 45-foot red-brick lighthouse.



**Toledo**

It's a restoration in progress, and the progress has been rough, but the Preservation Society keeps right on working to bring this Romanesque lighthouse back to its full glory.



**Vermilion**

This lighthouse was disassembled in 1929, but, happily, a full-size replica was built here in 1992.

# *Find out more about* LIGHTHOUSES

## 153 ASHTABULA HARBOR LIGHT

**Ashtabula Harbor, OH 44004**
**ashtabulalighthouse.com**

This lighthouse, first constructed in 1836, is more portable than most. The first version built was connected to a pier; 50 years later, a new one was built at a different pier, but when the Ashtabula River was widened, the lighthouse was left marooned in the bay. Thirty years later, it was moved from its island to a barge. The present lighthouse was built in 1905. In 1916, it was moved 1,750 feet to a concrete base. In 1927, it was rammed by a steamer and moved 6 inches, thus ending its travels—so far. Visits to the lighthouse are sometimes available via a floating dock during special events.

## 154 CEDAR POINT LIGHTHOUSE

**1 Cedar Point Drive,**
**Sandusky, OH 44871; 419-627-2350**
**cedarpoint.com/stay/lighthouse-point**

When Cedar Point amusement park bought an abandoned Coast Guard property in 1987, a derelict lighthouse was part of the deal. The first lighthouse in the area was built in 1839 and replaced in 1862. Other range lights were added later. After Cedar Point planners acquired the lighthouse, they decided to restore it and make it the centerpiece of Lighthouse Point, a camping-and-cabin resort within the park. The lighthouse is just for show; it's not open to the public.

ASHTABULA HARBOR LIGHT

## 155 CLEVELAND LIGHTHOUSES

These lighthouses are maintained by the U.S. Coast Guard and are closed to the public, but they're still popular with camera buffs and sightseers.

### 155A Cleveland East Entrance Lighthouse

**Located at the east end of a long breakwater forming the Cleveland harbor; GPS: 41.5101944°, -81.7155°**
**advkeen.co/clev_east_entrance**

### 155B Cleveland Harbor East Breakwater Light

**Located at the end of the breakwater at the east side of the entrance to the Cuyahoga River**
**GPS: 41.5102°, -81.7155°**
**advkeen.co/cleveland_harbor_east_breakwater**

### 155C Cleveland Harbor Main Entrance Light

**Located at the end of the breakwater on the west side of the entrance to the Cuyahoga River**
**GPS: 41.5089667°, -81.7177°**
**advkeen.co/cleveland_harbor_main_entrance**

## 156 CONNEAUT WEST BREAKWATER LIGHT

**Off Limestone Drive,**
**Conneaut, OH 44030**
**advkeen.co/conneaut_west_breakwater**

What do you do with a lighthouse when it goes out of service? This sleek, 60-foot tower was auctioned off twice after its decommissioning and is now in private hands. Located at the end of a free-standing breakwater, it is best seen from the public boat launch on Limestone Drive, but you'll need a telephoto lens to get a good photograph. It can also be seen from several points along Broad Street. The present structure was put into operation in 1934, replacing several earlier structures in different locations.

## 157 FAIRPORT HARBOR MARINE MUSEUM & LIGHTHOUSE

**129 Second Street,**
**Fairport Harbor, OH 44077**
**440-354-4825**
**advkeen.co/fairport_harbor_west_breakwater**

This is probably my favorite lighthouse in Ohio because it's open to the public and the keeper's house has a delightfully odd addition, a pilothouse from a Great Lakes vessel. Then there's the ghost cat . . . . The Fairport Harbor light isn't the prettiest you've ever seen, but you can climb the 69 iron steps to enjoy the breeze and the harbor view. In the attached former keeper's house, the museum focuses not just on the lighthouse but also on the rich history of the Great Lakes. One display features a local resident who was an engineer on the *Edmund Fitzgerald*. The pilothouse from the *Frontenac* has been added to the side of the museum, so visitors can walk directly aboard part of a real lake freighter. And that ghost cat? Its name is Sentinel, and it was the pet cat of a lighthouse keeper's wife. Its mummified remains are a creepy guard for the Founders' Room.

## 158 FAIRPORT HARBOR WEST BREAKWATER LIGHT

**Headlands Beach State Park,**
**9601 Headlands Road,**
**Mentor, OH 44060**
**GPS: 41.76815°, -81.2812°**
**fairportharborwestlighthouse.com**
**lighthousefriends.com/light.asp?ID=286**

All lighthouse lovers dream of living in one, don't they? Four people have tried to make the dream come true since

Fairport West was first auctioned off in 2005, but none have been successful yet. The current owner celebrated the lighthouse's 87th anniversary in 2012 by beginning a complete renovation of the classic four-square structure. In the meantime, the lighthouse remains in commission, with its automated light, foghorn, and a National Weather Service weather station all in service. There's no public access to Fairport West, but it can be seen from nearby Headlands Beach State Park, and from the Fairport Harbor Marine Museum and Lighthouse.

## 159 HURON LIGHTHOUSE

**North Main Street, Huron, OH 44839; 419-433-8487**
**advkeen.co/huron_harbor**
**advkeen.co/huron_parks**

It's easy to identify this 1930s lighthouse at a glance by its dramatic Art Deco design. You can walk out to this picturesque tower from the town park via a concrete fishing pier and a rocky sea wall. It's also visible from nearby Nickel Plate Beach. The first lighthouse was built here in 1835, and the present one was placed in service 101 years later. The lantern room was removed in 1972 when the light was automated. Solar panels were installed to power the new light, and its beacon can be seen for 12 miles.

## 160 LORAIN LIGHTHOUSE

**Jackalope dock: 301 Lakeside Avenue, Lorain, OH 44052; 440-204-2269 (boat tour reservations)**
**lorainlighthouse.com**

This lucky lighthouse has its own charitable foundation, which organizes fundraisers, applies for grants, sees to maintenance, and keeps the historic structure open for the public. The Lorain Lighthouse Foundation started out as a Save-the-Lighthouse Committee in the 1960s, and that's exactly what they did. June through September on Tuesday nights, sunset dinner cruises take passengers out from the Jackalope Lakeside Restaurant dock for a four-course meal with wine, followed by a lighthouse tour. Boat tours are also offered; check for a specific schedule. For a distant view of the lighthouse, walk the pier behind the Jackalope Lakeside Restaurant.

## 161 MARBLEHEAD LIGHTHOUSE

**110 Lighthouse Drive, Marblehead, OH 43440**
**419-734-4424**
**marbleheadlighthouseohio.org**

Though the lighthouse and keeper's house are part of Marblehead Lighthouse State Park, the Marblehead Lighthouse Historical Society maintains the museum in the picturesque and charming keeper's house. Nearby there's a replica of the 1876 U.S. Lifesaving Station, complete with a restored Coast Guard rescue boat on a launching railway. Also, don't miss the Wolcott House, home of a former keeper, which is also open for tours 2.7 miles away at 9999 East Bayshore Road. The museums are free, but if you want to climb the lighthouse itself, there's a $3 charge. Up the 77 steps, you can see several of Lake Erie's islands and the Cleveland shoreline.

## 162 PORT CLINTON LIGHTHOUSE

**West State Route 163, Port Clinton, OH 43452**
**419-504-8869**
**portclintonlighthouse.org**

It could have been a sad ending. The 26-foot Port Clinton Lighthouse, a replacement to an earlier one, was built in 1896 and saw service for some

30-odd years. It was moved from a breakwater to a marina in 1952, then later forgotten and left to deteriorate. In 2005, the owner talked to the city, and the Port Clinton Lighthouse Conservancy was formed. With a combination of grants and donations, the little structure was restored in 2014. Two years later, on an overcast August day, it was moved to Waterworks Park and raised by crane onto new concrete piers. The lighthouse is open limited hours Friday through Sunday.

## 163 SOUTH BASS ISLAND LIGHTHOUSE

**2368 Langram Road,**
**Put-in-Bay, OH 43456; 419-285-1800;**
**Tours: 614-292-8949**
**advkeen.co/south_bass**

Unlike most lighthouses, South Bass boasts a substantial redbrick 2½-story home with the 45-foot lighthouse attached at the back. Harry H. Riley was the first keeper in 1897, but the next year he was hospitalized with a mental illness. His wife became the keeper for the next two years. Today, a modern light tower is operated by the U.S. Coast Guard. Through an Ohio Sea Grant, the lighthouse itself is home to The Ohio State University's research and academic staff, which hosts tours during the summer. An 1899 barn and an 1897 oil house are also on the property. You can get a good look at the lighthouse from the ferries that service the island.

## 164 TOLEDO HARBOR LIGHTHOUSE

**Lighthouse Landing:**
**4441 North Summit, Toledo, OH 43611**
**419-691-3788**
**toledoharborlighthouse.org**

This could be the most unique lighthouse in Ohio. Four stories rise above a 20-foot crib base, making it 85 feet tall, with 4,000 square feet. It is built of buff brick with Romanesque arches and features a rolled-edge steel roof. The round metal tower at the top supports the lantern room. Completed in 1903, the lighthouse was automated in 1966 and is still lit today. Its original Fresnel lens has a new home at Quilter Lodge in Maumee Bay State Park. A renovation effort has been underway since 2003, led by the Toledo Harbor Lighthouse Preservation Society. The Society hosts regular fundraising events and occasionally offers boat tours. The best view of this lighthouse is from the water, so bring or rent a boat for an up-close look. You may see the lighthouse "ghost," which is actually a mannequin named Sarah, in an upper-story window.

## 165 VERMILION LIGHTHOUSE

**480 Main Street,**
**Vermilion, OH 44089; 440-204-2400**
**advkeen.co/vermilion**

You might call it "The Case of the Missing Lighthouse." The 34-foot tower visitors see today is a replica. The 1877 version was taken apart and moved away after storm damage in 1929. One of the brothers who first reported the storm damage, Ted Wakefield, always regretted the lighthouse's loss, and as an adult he headed the drive to build a replica on the grounds of the now-defunct Inland Seas Maritime Museum. A museum visitor eventually told a story that solved the mystery of the Missing Lighthouse. Olin W. Stevens, it turns out, once served as keeper at Vermilion. Later, on a new assignment, he was surprised to find himself keeping the same lighthouse in its new location. It had been reassembled on Lake Ontario at the St. Lawrence River and renamed the East Charity Shoal Light. The replica remains on the old museum grounds, but it is not open for tours.

VERMILION LIGHTHOUSE

NATIONAL MUSEUM OF THE GREAT LAKES, TOLEDO

## Ohio museums are nothing if not friendly.

Generally, if it isn't behind glass or a velvet rope, you can touch it. In fact, your kids can touch it too. Whether you like fire trucks, fine china, sports memorabilia, Civil War history, inaugural gowns, classic motorcycles, or working pliers carved from a single piece of wood, we've got a museum for you.

# Welcome to MUSEUMS

**About 300,000 Ohioans fought in the Civil War, contributing the largest number from any state.**

## *Find out more about* MUSEUMS

### 166 AMA MOTORCYCLE HALL OF FAME MUSEUM

**13515 Yarmouth Drive,
Pickerington, OH 43147; 614-856-2222
americanmotorcyclist.com/hof**

One of the cooler things about this museum is the covered priority parking, right next to the main entrance, for motorcycles. Wheel your ride into a first-class spot and stroll through the doors to immerse yourself in the history of motorcycling, much of which, surprisingly, took place in Ohio. The second-coolest thing is that American Motorcycle Association members are admitted free. Veterans are always given discounts, but their admission is free between Armed Forces Day (May 21) and Labor Day (September 5).

Here, motorcyclists have a place where they will always feel valued and welcome. On your visit be sure to see the Hall of Fame itself, where famous riders like Bessie Stringfield and Malcolm Smith are remembered, along with less-famous leaders in racing, touring, trail riding, and manufacturing. Besides rotating exhibits, the permanent exhibits include dozens of rare and famous bikes.

### 167 AMERICAN CIVIL WAR MUSEUM OF OHIO

**217 South Washington Street,
Tiffin, OH 44883; 419-455-9551
acwmo.org**

Hundreds of thousands of soldiers from Ohio fought for the Union effort. This museum examines the impact of the war on the lives of the common soldier, the difficult decisions of their leaders, and the hardships and losses suffered by those at home. Visitors can study the medicine used by field surgeons, the issues faced by prisoners, and the aftermath of America's first modern war. One story many Ohioans might not know is the role three Ohio companies played in the Great Locomotive Chase in Georgia, also known as Andrews' Raid.

### 168 AMERICAN SIGN MUSEUM

**1330 Monmouth Avenue,
Cincinnati, OH 45225; 513-541-6366
americansignmuseum.org**

Once upon a time, Tod Swormstedt edited *Signs of the Times* magazine. Facing a midlife crisis in 1999, he opened a sign museum inside an arts center. Still, that didn't solve the problem of what to do with his larger-than-life McDonald's and Holiday Inn signs. By 2012, the American Sign Museum had its own building. When you enter the exhibit space, you're surrounded by glowing neon, frenetically flashing signs, and more than a few oddities. See everything from beer and hardware-store signs to those that once adorned pharmacies, motels, and even funeral homes. Besides the signs themselves, the museum displays motors, cabinets, and the tools and paraphernalia of a sign maker. You can even order your own custom neon sign and watch it being

AMERICAN SIGN MUSEUM, CINCINNATI

built on-site by Neonworks. Don't forget to download a scavenger hunt for the kids before you go. The museum is open Wednesdays through Sundays, and it hosts events as well.

## 169 BIBLE WALK WAX MUSEUM

**500 Tingley Avenue, Mansfield, OH 44905; 419-524-0139**
**biblewalk.us**

Don't be intimidated by the idea of a Bible Walk. Whether you are religious or not, this museum is very much worth everyone's time. Set on the grounds of Diamond Hill Cathedral and framed by a peaceful garden, the Bible Walk was built in the 1980s by mostly volunteer labor and continues to expand every year. Its centerpieces are the 78 life-size wax dioramas of Bible scenes, some of which are animated. Everyone has a favorite, and mine is inspired by the 23rd Psalm. You might recognize a few of the people in the dioramas from Hollywood; the museum often repurposes wax figures it receives from other museums. You may therefore spot an old John Travolta or Tom Cruise figure standing amid the biblical scenes. There's also an extensive Christian art gallery at the museum, including oil paintings, folk art, wood carvings, and a rare-Bible collection. A dinner theater operates during the summer months.

## 170 BICYCLE MUSEUM OF AMERICA

**7 West Monroe Street, New Bremen, OH 45869**
**419-629-9249 or 419-629-2220 ext. 3808**
**bicyclemuseum.com**

If you grew up in Ohio, a state full of small towns, chances are you had a bicycle—and the rock-hard leg muscles to propel it. At this museum, you can explore the history of one of your earliest sports, from velocipedes to electric bikes and tricycles to three-wheelers meant for senior citizens. The museum's 800-bike collection, which rotates several times a year, includes a replica of the 1816 Draisine, a "walking machine" invented by German Karl van Drais. There are velocipedes, high-wheelers, police and military bicycles, "safety" bicycles popular with women, and bikes used by movie stars. Which would I prefer? That's easy, it's a 1998 Autobike Classic, meant for cyclists who never could figure out how to shift gears. Take your time on the three floors of this museum and let everyone in the family choose a favorite.

## 171 CANTON CLASSIC CAR MUSEUM

**123 6th Street Southwest, Canton, OH 44702; 330-455-3603**
**cantonclassiccar.org**

In its 40-car collection, this small gem of a museum showcases unusual and rare examples of historic automobiles. You can see Canton's own original and unrestored 1937 Ahrens-Fox Quad fire truck; a 1937 Packard hearse with hand-carved mahogany body panels; and a Canton-built car that has been called "possibly America's ugliest car," the 1922 Holmes Victoria Series. It also has steam engines and thousands of pieces of automobile paraphernalia, vintage advertisements, presidential artifacts, local history items, a vintage toy collection, and some unclassifiable oddities like an EX-LAX thermometer. It's the perfect museum for those who like to search out the unexpected, as well as the expected.

## 172 CENTRAL OHIO FIRE MUSEUM & LEARNING CENTER

**260 North 4th Street, Columbus, OH 43215-2511**
**614-464-4004**
**centralohiofiremuseum.com**

Children are welcome visitors to the restored 1908 Columbus Engine House #16, home of the Central Ohio Fire Museum & Learning Center. In age-appropriate groups, kids learn not to be afraid of fire gear. They can ring a fire bell and watch a firefighter slide down the pole. A play area includes the kids' own sliding pole, a fire truck cab with lights and sirens, and kid-size gear. Birthday parties can also be arranged. Adults, seniors, and those with handicaps can learn about fire safety too. Personalized tours are a big draw, not just for kids, but for their parents and grandparents. The engine house features original horse stalls, complete with hoof marks on the doors, and vintage hand-drawn and horse-drawn equipment. Meticulously appointed motorized equipment is also on display. On Fire Safety Way, visitors learn about fire prevention and safety and visit the Burned Room Display. The Columbus Heartmobile, which was the first mobile coronary care unit in the United States, is on permanent display here after being rescued from a scrapyard. Under the Museums for All program, anyone receiving SNAP benefits can visit for free or reduced rates. The engine house is on the National Register of Historic Places.

## 173 FIRST LADIES NATIONAL HISTORIC SITE

**205 South Market Avenue, Canton, OH 44702; 330-452-0876**
**firstladies.org**

In 1995, Canton resident Mary Regula asked First Lady Hillary Rodham Clinton why there wasn't a museum dedicated to first ladies. Clinton agreed that the idea was long overdue, and in 1998 she was the first person to access the new organization's website. Later that year, former First Lady Rosalyn Carter cut the ribbon to open the site in the former home of Ida Saxton and William McKinley. Today the museum is a national historic site and includes an education and research center nearby. The price of admission covers access to both buildings. Parking is free, but reservations are strongly recommended. Since the site operates under the National Park Service, NPS passes are accepted. The McKinley home is meticulously restored and presented in its full original glory, from President McKinley's enviable desk to the gorgeously layered period wallpaper in the front hall.

## 174 GLASS HERITAGE MUSEUM

**109 North Main Street, Fostoria, OH; 419-435-5077**
**fostoriaglass.com**

Because of its abundant supply of natural gas, Fostoria was seen as a good place for a glass factory in 1887. By the Roaring Twenties, the town had 13 of them. Some made workaday window glass, others made globes for some 60% of the period's kerosene lamps. The globes on display at this small museum range from heavy-handed pebbled glass to delicate three-layered prism glass. Some are lavishly decorated with glass ribbons and medallions; others are ethereal white-and-silver confections with delicately floating designs. Pretty glass tableware is also on display, part of the more than 1,000 items in the museum's collection.

## 175 THE JOHN & ANNIE GLENN MUSEUM

**72 West Main Street, New Concord, OH 43762**
**740-826-3305**
**johnglennhome.org**

This living-history museum, in the relocated home where Glenn grew up, presents three time periods that were important in the lives of Annie and John Glenn. In alternate years, costumed docents lead visitors through the house as it appeared in either 1937 (during the Great Depression), 1944 (during World War II), or 1962 (the year Glenn orbited Earth). I visited in a 1962 year, when a docent portraying Glenn's mother, Clara, described the family's fear and pride in Glenn's historic achievement. On the top floor of the home are Glenn's bedroom, a room dedicated to his wife, and other rooms full of memorabilia and information on Glenn's careers in the military, in space, and in politics. In an addition, visitors can watch a movie on the Glenns and visit a gift shop. Education is an essential part of the museum's mandate. Age-appropriate field guides are available to children, and student field trips are welcome. "Christmas at the House" programs for younger children give them a sense of an old-fashioned holiday. (See also John Glenn Astronomy Park on pages 167–168.)

## 176 LOU HOLTZ UPPER OHIO VALLEY HALL OF FAME & MUSEUM

**102 East Fifth Street,**
**East Liverpool, OH 43920**
**330-386-5443**
**louholtzhalloffame.com**

Legendary football coach Lou Holtz didn't like the idea of a hometown museum dedicated to him and his achievements, but he did like the idea of a Hall of Fame, so a compromise was reached. The historic First National Bank building became the institution's home, and the first honorees were inducted into the Upper Ohio Valley Hall of Fame in 1998. Inductees since then have included many Ohio Valley movers and shakers, as well as some nationally known names like Franco Harris, Regis Philbin, and Robert Urich. Besides information on Holtz's career, the museum features unique local-history pieces, like a vintage fire engine, a carousel horse from long-gone Rock Springs Park, and a sprawling model train setup built to look like East Liverpool. When you visit, notice the walk-in vault that served the First National Bank. Inside, you'll see memorabilia and information on 1930s gangster Pretty Boy Floyd, who was killed by local police a few miles from town.

## 177 MERRY-GO-ROUND MUSEUM

**301 Jackson Street,**
**Sandusky, OH 44870; 419-626-6111**
**merrygoroundmuseum.org**

Of course you can ride the merry-go-round here. Though it's not in original condition, the Allan Herschell carousel that is the centerpiece of this museum has been restored and filled with figures both vintage and modern. Stargazer (c. 1915), the lead horse, keeps his head to the sky and is a favorite choice for riders. The museum, opened in 1990 after a temporary exhibit proved wildly popular, features not only carousel animals but also Dentzel carving tools, memorabilia, and a restoration shop where visitors can watch artisans bring carousel animals and other folk art back to life. The museum raffles a hand-carved carousel horse every year as a fundraiser.

## 178 MOTTS MILITARY MUSEUM

**5075 South Hamilton Road,**
**Groveport, OH 43125**
**614-836-1500**
**mottsmilitarymuseum.org**

It started with Civil War memorabilia that Warren Motts kept in his basement. Today, his collection fills a sprawling campus and covers many American conflicts. In 2022, he added a memorial that honors 4,244 war dogs and their handlers. The museum also displays a large collection of 9/11 artifacts including the FDNY Ladder 18 fire truck that was buried when the second tower collapsed. A memorial garden is paved with bricks dedicated to individual veterans. Motts's mission is to bring to life the people behind the memorabilia. "See this uniform?" he asks kids. "Here's a picture of the guy who wore it. Here are his letters; here's his shaving kit. He's a real person." I have a personal connection to one piece of memorabilia there. Motts displays a Vietnam-era chopper, Huey Helicopter #66-17048, that was flown by a friend, former Army Warrant Officer Joe

Sepesy. A video of Joe talking about his old bird is on file at the museum.

## 179 MUSEUM OF CERAMICS

**400 East Fifth Street, East Liverpool, OH 43920**
**330-386-6001 or 800-600-7180**
**themuseumofceramics.com**

Just walking up to the building, a former post office, is a grand experience. The Beaux Arts edifice, which cost $100,000 to build in 1909, features domed ceilings, antique pendant lamps, a marble-and-terrazzo floor, and wrought iron fixtures. The museum tells the stories of some 300 potteries that once operated in this Pottery Capital of the World. Famous pottery imprints like Taylor, Smith & Taylor; Homer Laughlin; Knowles, Taylor & Knowles; and others fill the display cases. Sturdy Rockingham and yellow ware are shown alongside delicate Lotus Ware. In the cavernous basement are displays of pottery machinery, dioramas, and activity rooms. Upstairs, a theater provides space for community activities and an introductory film on the pottery industry. A recent addition is an outdoor mural featuring pottery, kilns, pottery workers, and Fiesta ware. The museum is closed during the winter months.

## 180 NATIONAL MUSEUM OF THE GREAT LAKES

**1701 Front Street, Toledo, OH 43605**
**419-214-5000**
**inlandseas.org**

Go ahead, stand at the wheel of the *Col. James M. Schoonmaker* and close your eyes. Imagine powering through waves, fighting storms, and delivering coal to Great Lakes cities. You're the master of your universe. Then open your eyes and look through the panoramic windows of the bridge, out to the water. Can't you just see it all? You may not actually be able to sail it, but you can walk through the *Schoonmaker* at the National Museum of the Great Lakes from May through October. The museum itself, on the edge of the Maumee River, sits amid a park full of marine artifacts that preserve Great Lakes stories and history. Committed to education, the museum hosts open houses for teachers, and it has a kids' club and a speakers' bureau.

## 181 NATIONAL ROAD & ZANE GREY MUSEUM

**8850 East Pike, Norwich, OH 43767**
**740-826-3305**
**nationalroadandzanegreymuseum.org**

Roadbuilding at the turn of the 19th century was a sweaty and dangerous enterprise, from felling trees by hand to shifting boulders and blasting hillsides. There's actually a student roadbuilding program at the museum to introduce kids to the process. The construction of the National Road, also called America's Main Street, is detailed in a ⅜-scale, 136-foot diorama at this fascinating museum. Allow plenty of time for the diorama, then more time to learn about Zane Grey, a former dentist from nearby Zanesville who wrote more than 80 books. He's best known for Westerns, but he is also the author of three books about his family, the pioneering Zanes, who included Revolutionary War heroine Betty Zane. Grey's study, including his original desk, has been re-created in the museum, and some manuscripts and memorabilia are also on display. The museum's attractions also include a display of local pottery.

## 182 NATIONAL UNDERGROUND RAILROAD FREEDOM CENTER

**50 East Freedom Way, Cincinnati, OH 45202; 513-333-7500 freedomcenter.org**

The Ohio River was, of course, an important piece of the Underground Railroad prior to the Civil War. Once across, escaped slaves were out of slave territory but not out of danger. The Rankin family of Cincinnati, for instance, helped more than 2,000 people to freedom from their home on Liberty Hill, overlooking the river. This museum chronicles the stories of the escapees and their "conductors" along the secret, illegal "railroad" to freedom. The Center operates a teen docent program in which local high schoolers learn to engage with history and develop leadership skills. It also provides an Implicit Bias Learning Lab, which it offers to organizations. Beyond that, the organization operates a free genealogy center and is active in the Freedom Stations Program, which links with other Underground Railroad sites. It is also involved in modern abolitionism, which works to combat worldwide slavery today.

## 183 OHIO GLASS MUSEUM & GLASS BLOWING STUDIO

**124 W. Main Street, Lancaster, OH 43130; 740-687-0101 ohioglassmuseum.org**

Isaac Collins and partners founded what would become Anchor Hocking in Lancaster in 1905, ensuring that Lancaster would become one of the premier glassmaking cities in the state. The Ohio Glass Museum was founded in 2002 to preserve the history of glassmaking and educate the public in the art. Displays include commercial glass pieces such as insulators, traffic signals and vehicle lights, lanterns, art pieces, and tableware. Glassmaking equipment is also on display. Demonstrations in making hot glass are part of the museum experience. Classes are offered regularly in fused glass or hot glass, and private classes are available for large groups.

## 184 PACKARD MUSEUMS

### 184A America's Packard Museum

**420 South Ludlow Street, Dayton, OH 45402; 937-226-1710 americaspackardmuseum.org**

Operating in a restored 1917 Art Deco Packard dealership, this museum is dedicated to preserving Packard history. Along with automobile memorabilia, more than 50 cars are on display, representing models from the 1900s to the 1950s. Many of the Packards are convertibles, and there's also a carefully preserved 1918 Model E Army truck that still participates in military parades and car shows. The museum's education arm teaches schools and clubs about design, engineering, history, culture, and preservation. The museum is also an event venue that can handle up to 250 people. All transportation clubs are welcome.

PACKARD HOOD ORNAMENT

### 184B National Packard Museum

1899 Mahoning Avenue Northwest, Warren, OH 44483; 330-394-1899
packardmuseum.org

In Warren, home of the Packard, this small, nicely appointed museum features one-of-a-kind Packard automobiles, like the last-known Warren-built car—the 1927 Sterling Knight—and a 1941 One Eighty Touring limousine owned by Mrs. J. W. Packard. My favorite is a pristine 1900 Model B Packard that's basically a frame, a seat, a steering handle with horn, and a foot-operated chime. Memorabilia includes Packard banners, other period artifacts, and displays on the Packard Electric Company. The museum has a busy schedule of events that includes an annual motorcycle exhibit, a "Corvettes and Classics" car show, parties, lectures, and seminars.

## 185 PRESIDENTIAL MUSEUMS & LIBRARIES

Here's another reason Ohio considers itself at the heart of it all—eight presidents have called it home. Presidential libraries and museums are thick here, and all are popular among fans of US history and politics. Among them are the homes from which James Garfield and Warren G. Harding conducted their front-porch campaigns, and the sprawling estate of Major General, Congressman, Governor, and President Rutherford B. Hayes.

### 185A James A. Garfield Monument

Lakeview Cemetery,
12316 Euclid Avenue,
Cleveland, OH 44106; 216-421-2665
lakeviewcemetery.com/visit/james-a-garfield-memorial

### 185B James A. Garfield National Historic Site

8095 Mentor Avenue,
Mentor, OH 44060
440-255-8722
nps.gov/jaga

### 185C Rutherford B. Hayes Presidential Library & Museums

Spiegel Grove, Fremont, OH 43420
419-332-2081
rbhayes.org

### 185D Ulysses S. Grant Birthplace

1551 Route 232, Moscow, OH 45153
513-497-0492
advkeen.co/grant_birthplace

### 185E Ulysses S. Grant Home

219 E Grant Avenue,
Georgetown, OH 45121
877- 372-8177
usgrantboyhoodhome.org

### 185F Ulysses S. Grant School

508 S. Water Street,
Georgetown, OH 4512
877-372-8177
ohiohistory.org/visit/browse-historical-sites/u-s-grant-boyhood-home-schoolhouse

### 185G Warren G. Harding Home and Museum

380 Mt. Vernon Avenue,
Marion, OH 43302
740-387-9630
hardingpresidentialsites.org

### 185H Warren G. Harding Memorial

966-870 Delaware Avenue,
Marion, OH 43302
800-600-6894 or 740-387-9630
hardingpresidentialsites.org

### 185I William Henry Harrison Tomb

41 Cliff Road, North Bend, OH 45052
844-288-7709
advkeen.co/harrison_tomb

### 185J Harrison-Symmes Memorial Foundation Museum

**112 S. Miami Avenue, Cleves, OH 45002; 513-301-0054**
**hsmfmuseum.org**

### 185K William McKinley Presidential Library & Museum

**800 McKinley Monument Drive Northwest, Canton, OH 44708**
**330-455-7043**
**mckinleymuseum.org**

### 185L William Howard Taft National Historic Site

**2038 Auburn Avenue, Cincinnati, OH 45219; 513-684-3262**
**nps.gov/wiho**

## 186 ROCK & ROLL HALL OF FAME

**1100 Rock and Roll Boulevard, Cleveland, OH 44114**
**216-781-ROCK (7625)**
**rockhall.com**

"Sensory overload" is a frequent comment of visitors to this world-famous shrine of rock and roll. Why Cleveland? Because they fought hard for it, and they've been enthusiastically partying hard ever since. Just the groundbreaking, for instance, featured performances by Chuck Berry, Pete Townsend, and Ruth Brown. Johnny Cash, Aretha Franklin, and Booker T. & the M.G.'s came to the opening. Once a year, the Rock hosts a very loud celebration for that year's five inductees into the Hall of Fame. To date, nearly 400 rock and roll performers and influencers have been inducted as official participants in rock and roll history. Even fans can take part in the action by renting the Rock for a wedding, prom, or party.

## 187 WARTHER MUSEUM & GARDENS

**331 Karl Avenue, Dover, OH 44622**
**330-505-6003**
**thewarthermuseum.com**

It's a visit many Ohioans make sooner or later because word-of-mouth draws them. "You won't believe what this guy did!" is enough to bring tourists, and they're always glad they came. Ernest Warther was a woodcarver, plain and simple, and what he did with his talent was plainly, simply amazing. He carved in ebony, ivory, and walnut. His incredibly ornate carving of the Lincoln funeral train is probably the most famous piece, but no less impressive are the hundreds of working wooden pliers scattered through the collection. He carved, and his descendants still carve, each pair from a single piece of wood. He also collected more than 5,000 Native American arrowheads, and his wife, Frieda, collected 73,000 buttons, which she arranged in quilt motifs all over the walls of her Button Cottage. The Swiss-style Dave Warther Arboretum is popular for events, and the museum itself offers a candlelight-dinner tour for groups. Educators are welcome free of charge during a week every summer and can customize tours for their students. Children are treated to a Christmas-tree-decorating workshop. Veterans are admitted free on Memorial Day Weekend.

## 188 YOUNGSTOWN HISTORICAL CENTER OF INDUSTRY AND LABOR

**151 West Wood Street,**
**Youngstown, OH 44503 330-941-1314**
**ohiohistory.org/visit/museum-and-site-locator/youngstown-historical-center-of-industry-and-labor**

Iron and steel mills are still a sore subject in the Mahoning Valley, once a thriving industrial community that saw hard times after wholesale mill closures in the 1980s. A rich legacy survives at this museum, though. Immigration brought factory workers into the area's working-class neighborhoods, and their stories are documented in photographs and in a re-creation of a company house. The tools and clothing of steelworkers are on display. Visitors can also see reproductions of a mill locker room and a blooming mill, where steel ingots were made. Stories of the different mills' "last heats" are also told.

**Cleveland is the home of the first electric traffic light in the United States. It was installed on August 5, 1914, at the intersection of East 105th and Euclid.**

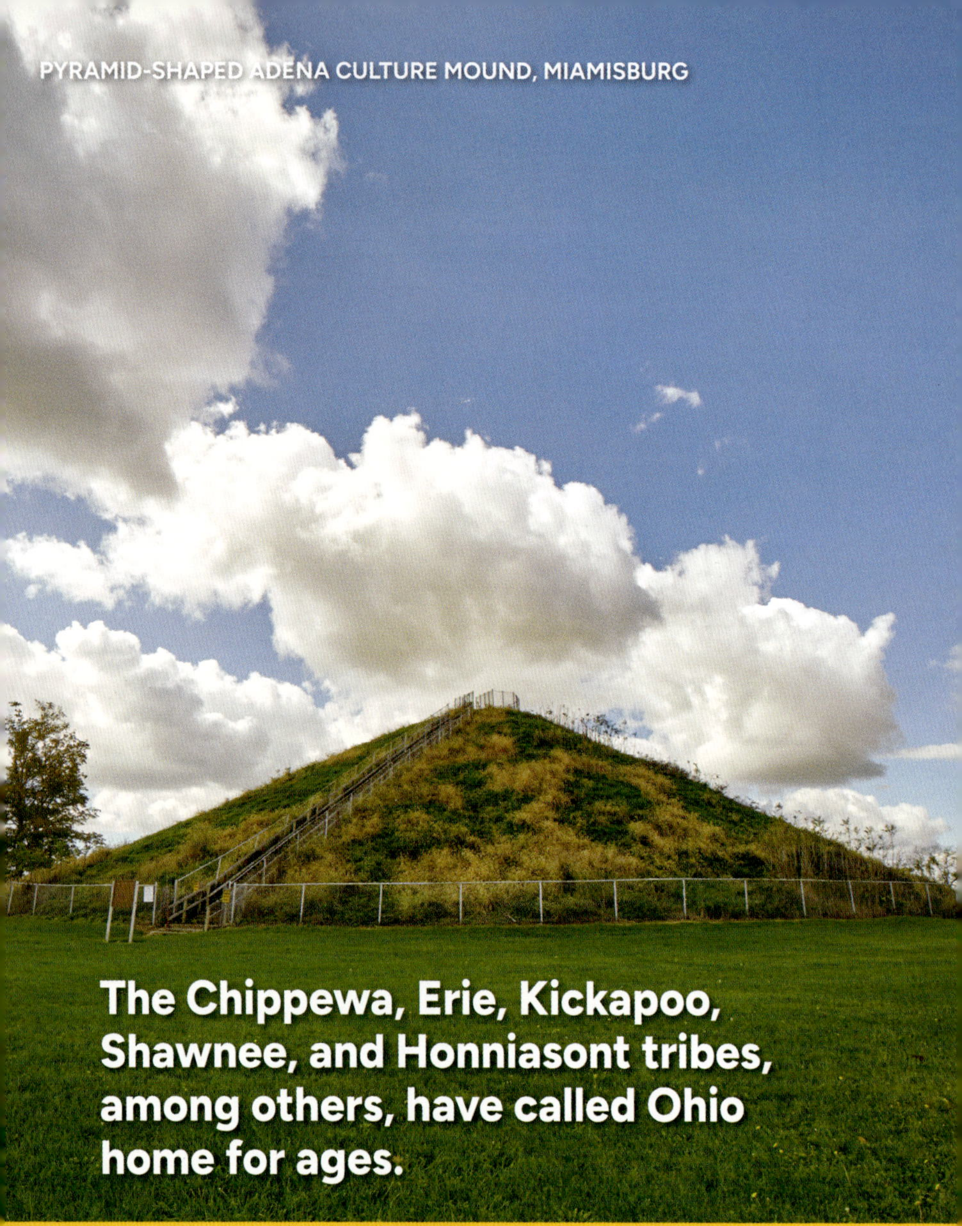

PYRAMID-SHAPED ADENA CULTURE MOUND, MIAMISBURG

**The Chippewa, Erie, Kickapoo, Shawnee, and Honniasont tribes, among others, have called Ohio home for ages.**

In fact, the word *Ohio* itself means "large river" in the Seneca language. Native Americans first arrived in Ohio more than 12,000 years ago, but by the mid-1800s, most of Ohio's populations had succumbed to introduced diseases or had been forcibly displaced to reservations in Kansas and Oklahoma. Today, Native Americans once again live in Ohio, and evidence of their continuing influence abounds—from the state's place names, earthworks, and historic sites to impacts on music, literature, and beyond.

# Welcome to NATIVE AMERICAN CULTURE

**189 CHIEF LEATHERLIPS MONUMENT** .......... 118

**Dublin**

His word was as strong as leather, but it led to his death after he signed the Treaty of Greenville.

**190 FORT ANCIENT EARTHWORKS & NATURE PRESERVE** .......... 119

**Oregonia**

Wright State University students conduct digs here every summer. Join them in exploring the Moorehead Circle, a woodhenge, in the park's North Fort.

**191 GREAT SERPENT MOUND** .......... 119

**Peebles**

It might have something to do with an eclipse, it might be a burial ground, or it might just be a really big piece of prehistoric art. The shaped effigy mound stretches more than 1,300 feet.

**192 HOPEWELL CULTURE NATIONAL HISTORICAL PARK** .......... 120

**Chillicothe**

The Mound City burial grounds within this park contain not only Native American remains but also copper figurines, hunting equipment, and other artifacts.

**193 LEO PETROGLYPHS & NATURE PRESERVE** .......... 120

**Ray**

The projecting roof of a stone shelter preserves figurative etchings of people and animals.

**194 POWWOWS** .......... 120

**Statewide**

Ohio powwows can be intensely patriotic and dramatic and, at the same time, provide as much fun as a country fair.

## *Find out more about*
# NATIVE AMERICAN CULTURE

### 189 CHIEF LEATHERLIPS MONUMENT

**7377 Riverside Drive,**
**Dublin, OH 43016**
**roadsideamerica.com/story/9791**

When Ohio schoolchildren learn about Wyandot Chief Leatherlips in Ohio history class, they tend to snicker over the name, but it's actually a tragic story. As a chief, he encouraged peace with European settlers, going so far as to sign the 1795 Treaty of Greenville, which ceded most of Ohio to settlers. He believed it was best for his people to coexist with them. His tribe sentenced him to death in 1810, officially for witchcraft, but actually for his political position. Leatherlips refused to go back on his word to keep the peace, and he was executed by tomahawk at the command of a committee headed by his brother. He's remembered today in a quirky monument at Scioto Park in Dublin. A sphinx-like 12-foot head made of artfully placed limestone slabs overlooks a hillside near the site of his death. The effigy, designed and built by Ralph Helmick in 1990, is reminiscent of the Crazy Horse monument in South Dakota. It's possible to walk out onto Leatherlips' head for an up-close and personal look at this statue honoring the famous peacemaker.

CHIEF LEATHERLIPS MONUMENT, DUBLIN

GREAT SERPENT MOUND, PEEBLES

## 190 FORT ANCIENT EARTHWORKS & NATURE PRESERVE

**6123 State Route 350,
Oregonia, OH 45054
513–932–4421 or 800–283–8904
fortancient.org**

History is not just preserved here; it's palpable and accessible for everyone, from kindergarteners to lifelong learners. The National Historic Landmark operates customized tours that offer classes, family groups, and history buffs a chance to learn about the history of the pre-Columbian Hopewell and Fort Ancient Native American cultures. This is the largest hilltop mound complex in North America, and archaeologists believe it was an important ceremonial center used by Native Americans from all over the continent. Some of the earthen mounds are 23 feet high; others are small and serve as astronomical alignments. The park's trails lead to lookout points, prairies, and what might have been a dock on the Little Miami River.

## 191 GREAT SERPENT MOUND

**3850 State Route 73,
Peebles, OH 45660; 800-752-2757
ohiohistory.org/visit/browse-historical-sites/serpent-mound**

Building a monument wasn't so easy in pre-Columbian times. Native Americans didn't have steel or concrete to construct this serpent effigy, so they used the material they had at hand—dirt. Workers piled enough dirt to build a three-foot-high snake with an open mouth and coiled tail; altogether, it's 1,348 feet long. Three burial mounds are adjacent. Scientists speculate that the snake effigy was used for ceremonial purposes. The mound may have been important in Native American cosmology, since its shape also is aligned astronomically. Visitors today can come up with their own theories, as they walk the paths around the mound and visit the nearby Serpent Mound Museum.

## 192 HOPEWELL CULTURE NATIONAL HISTORICAL PARK

**16062 State Route 104, Chillicothe, OH 45601; 740-774-1126**
**nps.gov/hocu**

We learn a lot about the history of America in school, but what was life like here before Europeans arrived? The **Scioto River Valley** in southwest Ohio was a busy place for Native Americans 2,000 years ago. People of the Hopewell Culture flourished here, leaving behind mysterious and monumental earthen enclosures. Six separate groups of earthworks are preserved and partially rebuilt in this historical park surrounding Chillicothe: **High Bank Works, Hopeton Earthworks, Hopewell Mound Group, Mound City Group, Seip Earthworks,** and **Spruce Hill Earthworks.** Five are open to the public, where visitors can see reconstructed mounds and learn about the social, spiritual, ceremonial, political, and economic lives of the Hopewell people. The park's visitor center, at the Mound City Group just north of Chillicothe, includes artifact exhibits and information about tours.

## 193 LEO PETROGLYPHS & NATURE PRESERVE

**400 Park Road, Ray, OH 45672**
**800-860-0144**
**advkeen.co/leo_petroglyphs**

Ancient Native Americans not only built massive earthworks in Ohio, but they also produced art that has survived for millennia. This tiny preserve in south-central Ohio consists of a half-mile trail that leads inquisitive hikers along a sandstone gorge and past small waterfalls to a rock shelter. Here, people of the Fort Ancient culture drew dozens of petroglyphs that include human figures and footprints, plus images of birds, fish, and animal tracks.

## 194 POWWOWS

**Statewide**

Music, color, regalia, food, and heritage combine to educate and entertain visitors to a powwow. Performers with Native American heritage provide a thrilling and inspiring spectacle that serves to remind us all of the rich and complex history of America's first inhabitants.

Many powwows begin with a grand entrance parade. Some include contests in drumming, dancing, singing, and storytelling; others are noncompetitive. It's worthwhile to attend just to see the dancers' regalia. Women and men typically perform separately in traditional, ceremonial, and modern forms, including the Hoop Dance, Gourd Dance, Snake Dance, and Bread Dance. Some powwows are inter-tribal, while others are sponsored by just one or a few tribes. There may be a charitable component, with proceeds going to a local food pantry or worthy cause. Veterans are honored guests.

### 194A AuGlaize Village Powwow & Gourd Dance

**AuGlaize Village & Farm Museum, 12296 Krouse Road, Defiance, OH 43512**
**sites.google.com/site/auglaizevillagemuseum**

### 194B Baby Bison Days

**Boss Bison Ranch, 45701 Unionvale Road, Cadiz, OH 43907; 740-312-1940**
**advkeen.co/baby_bison_days**

**194C Great Mohican Pow-wow**
Mohican Reservation
Campgrounds & Canoeing,
23270 Wally Road,
Loudonville, OH 44842
800-766-2267
mohicanpowwow.com

**194D Harvest Moon Gathering**
The Ridge Museum,
14430 Flint Ridge Road,
Glenford, OH 43739; 740-787-2869
calendar.powwows.com/events
/harvest-moon-gathering-pow-wow

**194E Honoring Our Ancestors: 13th Annual Intertribal Powwow**
UELN & Ashtabula County
Antique Engine Club,
4026 US Highway 322,
Williamsfield, OH 44093
440-536-2213

**194F Honoring the Traditions**
Buffalo Creek Retreat,
8708 Hubbard Valley Road,
Seville, OH 44273; 330-635-7634

**194G Honoring Tradition: An Eastern Woodland Native American Celebration**
Fairfield County Fairgrounds
AAA Building,
157 East Fair Avenue,
Lancaster, OH 43130; 740-304-9720

**194H Woodland Gathering**
153, Zanesfield, OH 43360
937-441-1565
calendar.powwows.com/events/8th
-annual-native-woodland-gathering

**The Hopewell Ceremonial Earthworks were designated as a UNESCO World Heritage Site in 2023. The site includes eight locations that were built by the Hopewell Culture around 1,600–2,000 years ago.**

FIELD OF CORN, DUBLIN

**Every state has its own strange and wonderful, out-of-the-way corners not mentioned in any museum or designated with an official landmark.**

Going on a tour of these places might expose a worthwhile bit of history or reveal a unique piece of outsider art. Or it might just be a fun place to go for a day trip. Either way, taking the time to go off the beaten path will give you a more profound sense of what Ohio is all about.

*Welcome to*

# ODDS & ENDS

## 195 ANNIE OAKLEY, FRANK BUTLER GRAVESITES........ 125

**Versailles**

It's possible that Annie isn't buried under her gravestone, but people still leave flowers there today, in Brock Cemetery.

## 196 B.A. SWEETIE CANDY COMPANY.............. 125

**Cleveland**

If you've got a world-class sweet tooth and have a hankering to visit the largest candy store in America, it's right here in Ohio.

## 197 BLUE ROCK STATION......... 125

**Philo**

You might not like the idea of a house built of recycled tires, pop bottles, and old barn wood, but if you're at all curious, the Warmkes would love to show you how it's done.

## 198 COLUMBUS WASHBOARD FACTORY... 126

**Logan**

How to work and how to play—that's what you can learn at the only remaining washboard factory in the United States.

## 199 CORNHENGE......................... 126

**Dublin**

There's really no explanation for a place like Cornhenge. You just have to go and see it for yourself.

## 200 THE J. M. SMUCKER COMPANY STORE AND CAFÉ.............................. 126

**Orrville**

Everyone knows Smucker's, right? They make jams and jellies. You might be surprised to know they make a lot of other products, too, which you can buy at their store and café.

## 201 LONGABERGER BASKET BUILDING............. 127

**Newark**

It's only a drive-by attraction now, and a sad one at that, but it might be worth a trip if you have fond memories of Longaberger basket parties.

## 202 OHIO STATE REFORMATORY...... 127

**Mansfield**

A former state prison is spooky by definition, and this one doesn't disappoint, but it also has Hollywood cachet, as the setting for *The Shawshank Redemption* movie.

## 203 PIATT CASTLES.................. 127

**West Liberty**

They aren't actually castles, but they are fabulous and imposing family homes preserved for the love of history in rural Ohio.

**Alcoholics Anonymous was founded in Akron.**

### 204 SALTPETRE CAVE STATE NATURE PRESERVE ........... 128

**Logan**

If you're looking for nature in all of its solitary splendor, this is the place to find it. To visit the cave complex on 14 isolated acres in a hidden corner of the Hocking Hills, you'll need a state permit.

### 205 SMITH CEMETERY STATE NATURE PRESERVE ........... 128

**Plain City**

The story here isn't size, as less than an acre is preserved. The story is in the people who lived and died here.

### 206 SPANGLER CANDY WORLD..................... 128

**Bryan**

Do you know someone who has always wanted a Dum Dums T-shirt of their very own? This is the place to get it, at the home of Dum Dums lollipops.

### 207 THURBER HOUSE................ 128

**Columbus**

The family of American humorist James Thurber lived here during his college years, and today it serves as a museum and a literary center for readers and writers.

### 208 USS *COD* SUBMARINE MEMORIAL............................. 129

**Cleveland**

The *Cod,* built in 1942, served in the Pacific during WWII. Touring it today, you get a unique sense of how difficult life could be for a submariner on a cramped, hot underwater vessel that survived by evading threats and hiding between missions.

# Find out more about ODDS & ENDS

## 195 ANNIE OAKLEY, FRANK BUTLER GRAVESITES

**Brock Cemetery,**
**11775–11791 Greenville Saint Marys Road,**
**Versailles, OH 45380**
**advkeen.co/annie_oakley**
**advkeen.co/oakley_grave**

Signs leading to Brock Cemetery are present on more than one road in the area, and an Ohio Historical Marker stands with the gravestones, which simply read, "At Rest." The couple, who were married 50 years, died within weeks of each other. Rumor has it that Annie's cremains are actually preserved in one of her trophies inside Butler's coffin. Annie Oakley, who beat sharpshooter Frank Butler in a shooting contest when she was 15 and then married him a year later, was born near Versailles. Her father taught her to shoot, and she later supported her mother and siblings by hunting after her father died. She and Butler became stars of Buffalo Bill's Wild West Show in 1885 and were world famous. Oakley, a champion for women's rights, once volunteered a company of 50 female sharpshooters to President William McKinley for the Spanish-American War.

## 196 B.A. SWEETIE CANDY COMPANY

**6770 Brookpark Road,**
**Cleveland, OH 44129; 216-739-2244**
**sweetiescandy.com**

Imagine 5,500 different kinds of candy from 190 candy manufacturers, all for sale in one giant store that draws more than half a million visitors each year. That's what you'll find at Sweetie's, which calls itself the largest candy store in America. You can buy candy by the piece, by the scoop, or by the bag. Do you need 30 pounds? They sell master cases, just for people like you. Sweetie's does a lot of wholesale candy sales, too, which accounts for those master cases. You could overdose on sugar just by walking down the long aisles of candy racks. Jelly Belly, Haribo, Hershey, M&M, Pez, Tootsie Rolls, Wrigley, Goobers, Raisinets, Butterfingers, and more are all here. You can even find old-fashioned names like Hi-Chews and Slo-Poke and Chiclets. Sweetie's makes popcorn in five different flavors, and they're very proud of their own Poop-tastic candy. There's also a Sweeties Soda Shoppe that seats 150, with 36 flavors of ice cream made on-site. Outside, there's a 36-hole miniature golf course with its own concession stand where you can buy snacks and even more candy. What else is there to say? Mmmmmmmmm!

## 197 BLUE ROCK STATION

**1190 Virginia Ridge Road,**
**Philo, OH 43771; 740-674-4300**
**bluerockstation.com**

Annie and Jay Warmke started building what they call the Earthship in 1996 and have lived in it since 2004. Starting with 1,200 tires brought from an illegal dump, they rammed the tires full of dirt and used them to construct the walls of the house. Other walls, both in the main house and in outbuildings, are built of straw bales, reclaimed wood, glass and plastic bottles, or aluminum cans. The couple's goal in building the Earthship was to combine engineering, art, and recycling as part of sustainable practice. They also use homemade solar collectors and rainwater collectors. Because so many people have expressed interest in their project, the Warmkes host Saturday tour days several times a year (see website for dates), conduct regular workshops in sustainable living, and accept interns who live and work on the property.

## 198 COLUMBUS WASHBOARD FACTORY

**4 East Main Street, Logan, OH 43138**
**740-380-3828**
**columbuswashboard.com**

Touring a washboard factory might not be high on your day-trip wish list, but give it a chance. Here you'll see some of the company's original manufacturing equipment in daily use. Each washboard is still made mostly by hand, one at a time. The surfaces of the boards can be spiral metal, galvanized, stainless steel, brass, glass, cork, chalk, or mirror. You can use them for handwashing at home, in camp, or while deployed. They're very popular for decorative use. Oh, you can also use them to play bluegrass music, especially at the annual Washboard Musical Festival held Father's Day weekend in Logan. Musical washboards come in many sizes, shapes, and materials and can even be fashioned in guitar shapes. The factory store also sells soaps and salves, laundry items like drying racks, crafts supplies, and Fostoria glassware.

## 199 CORNHENGE

**4995 Rings Road, Dublin, OH 43017**
**614-410-4550**
**advkeen.co/field_corn**
**advkeen.co/cornhenge**

The official name for this art installation is *Field of Corn (with Osage Orange Trees)*, and it's also known as Frantz Park. Locals reportedly call it the "seement corn," and they're actually right. These are 6-foot sculptures of shucked ears of corn made of white concrete, rising right out of the ground in tidy rows. There are 109 ears of corn in four slightly different shapes. Each weighs 1,500 pounds. The installation was commissioned by the Dublin Arts Council in 1995 to honor a local farmer, Sam Frantz, who developed several hybrid corn varieties. The Osage orange trees, by the way, are off in one corner of the field. Cornhenge, as it is commonly known, was not a popular art installation at first, but people have come to appreciate it. The site gets a lot of visitors, and weddings have even been held here.

## 200 THE J. M. SMUCKER COMPANY STORE & CAFÉ

**333 Wadsworth Road,**
**Orrville, OH 44667; 330-684-1500**
**jmsmucker.com/smuckers-corporate/smuckers-store-orrville**

In a nod to its founding as a cider mill, the entry to Smucker's Store and Café is lined by apple trees. Inside the sprawling store you can find all their products, arranged in sections. It's surprisingly entertaining to browse the shelves, picking out old favorites like Uncrustables and new unfamiliar ones like ice-cream syrups. Besides the Smucker's brand of jams, jellies, and peanut butter, they produce other familiar names like Hostess snack cakes, Eagle Brand milk, Robin Hood products, Folger's, Dunkin Donuts Coffee, and much more. They also manufacture pet foods.

## 201 LONGABERGER BASKET BUILDING

**1500 East Main Street,**
**Newark, OH 43055-8847**
**advkeen.co/largest_basket**
**advkeen.co/longaberger**

It's been a roadside icon in Ohio since it was built in 1997—the seven-story building that looks like a market basket. It was the headquarters of the Longaberger Company, which sold pricey handmade baskets through direct sales at home parties. After the founder's death, the company was sold and the building eventually abandoned when employees were moved to other quarters. Though the property has been sadly neglected, restoration plans are being made by a new owner.

## 202 OHIO STATE REFORMATORY

**100 Reformatory Road,**
**Mansfield, OH 44905; 419-522-2644**
**mrps.org**

You can take a self-guided tour of the former state prison, but who would want to? It's much safer, given the reformatory's dark history and reputation for ghosts, to join a tour group. There are several guided tours from which to choose, including four paranormal tours that can be taken with ghost-hunting equipment like EMF meters. Since the reformatory was famously used to film *Air Force One* and *The Shawshank Redemption* movies, you can do things like follow the Shawshank Trail from the reformatory to 14 filming sites in and around Mansfield, marked by handy "Movie Site" posters. Special events held at the reformatory include a fun run, charity events, and a tattoo festival. In the fall, special Escape to Blood Prison tours are available. Dinners for conferences and fundraisers for up to 400 can be arranged, though they don't allow weddings or receptions.

## 203 PIATT CASTLES

**Mac-A-Cheek Castle:**
**10051 Township Road 47,**
**West Liberty, OH 43357**
**937-465-2821**
**piattcastles.org**

Since 1912, when William McCoy Piatt opened a few rooms of Mac-A-Cheek for tours, these iconic castles, built by brothers Abram and Donn Piatt, have fascinated visitors. Nearby Mac-O-Chee Castle is now privately owned and no longer allows tours, but the Piatt family still maintains Mac-A-Cheek as a repository of history, as well as object lessons for the importance of family lore. They try to make tours "less about us" and more about the visitors' own family stories and mementos. The castle is open April through October for tours of artifacts, photographs, period furnishings, and exhibits. Their nonprofit foundation provides multiple educational programs for students, focusing on Ohio history, geology, literature, math, and architecture through projects, crafts, games, storytelling, and theater. There are also camps every summer that feature the castle as a springboard for imagination and theater.

## 204 SALTPETRE CAVE STATE NATURE PRESERVE

**Near Hocking Hills State Park,
25994 Big Pine Road,
Rockbridge, OH 43149; 614-265-6561
advkeen.co/saltpetre_cave
advkeen.co/saltpetre_cave_2
Permit application: naturepreserves.ohiodnr.gov/Portals/0/Forms/dnap/permits/ApplicationAccessPermit.pdf**

One of the best-kept secrets of the ODNR is this seldom-visited nature preserve in the middle of a busy tourist area; access is only available with a permit (apply at least 14 days in advance). The recess caves here are named for the potassium nitrate, or saltpetre, that was once mined for gunpowder manufacture. They are located on 14 acres with a short trail system providing access. Trails through the preserve are well kept and include stairs when needed. Saltpetre is still visible on some of the cave ceilings. A couple of the caves are more than 100 feet deep. You'll need to bring a flashlight and watch your footing to get all the way inside them.

## 205 SMITH CEMETERY STATE NATURE PRESERVE

**4400 Boyd Road,
Plain City, OH 43064; 614-265-6561
advkeen.co/smith_cemetery**

The wet-and-swampy Darby Plains around Smith Cemetery were considered good only for wildflowers and bur oaks by early settlers, who bypassed the area quickly while swatting at clouds of mosquitoes. Farmers from New England eventually drained the plains for cropland and obliterated much of the tallgrass prairie. Soon the original flora survived mostly in tiny family cemeteries like this one, donated to the state in the early 1800s by Samuel Smith Jr. The site is less than an acre in area but is very much worth a short visit to commune with the ghosts of long-vanished pioneers.

## 206 SPANGLER CANDY WORLD

**131 South Main Street,
Bryan, OH 43506
419-636-3553 or 800-628-2639
spanglercandyworld.com**

The good news is that admission is free. The better news is that Spangler Candy World is a kid-centric place with plenty of activities that the kids won't even realize are educational. There are touchless video games, STEM activities, and some very cool robotic arms that help sort candy. The Candy World Theater offers a virtual tour of the Spangler factory. There are photo opportunities scattered around, including a Sweetheart Chapel. There are Learn and Play Kiosks and displays of historic artifacts. This is the home of a candy you've known and loved all your life, beginning with Saf-T-Pops. They also make Dum Dums lollipops (12 million per day), Spangler Candy Canes (2.7 million per day), and Spangler Circus Peanuts. A party room can seat up to 20 children. School tours are offered and include curriculum-based worksheets. Candy World is open Mondays through Saturdays.

## 207 THURBER HOUSE

**77 Jefferson Avenue,
Columbus, OH 43215; 614-464-1032
thurberhouse.org**

Visitors to this beautifully restored 1873 home are encouraged to consider themselves guests of author James

Thurber's family in some of the rooms. You can sit on the furniture, play the piano, and be comfortably at home. Two floors contain period furnishings, family items, and Thurber memorabilia donated by the writer's brother, Robert. Tours of the house include anecdotes of the ghosts Thurber wrote about in *My Life* and *Hard Times*. On the third floor is an apartment reserved for visiting writers and artists. Outdoors, a reading garden includes statues inspired by Thurber cartoons. The house is open on Tuesday, Thursday, Saturday, and Sunday from 1 to 4 p.m. Thurber House is also a community literary arts center that offers adult and youth writing programs, lectures, author residencies, and resources for writers.

## 208 USS *COD* SUBMARINE MEMORIAL

**1089 E. 9th St., North Coast Harbor, Cleveland, OH 44114; 440-832-9722**
**usscod.org**
**advkeen.co/cod_submarine**

The *Cod* is a remarkable example of World War II diesel submarines. It sank the Japanese destroyer *Karukaya* with a Mark IV Torpedo Data Computer in 1944, and it was involved in the only international submarine-to-submarine rescue in history when, in 1945, it rescued the crew of Dutch submarine *O-19,* which was grounded on a reef. Be sure to see the sub's restored, fully operational mechanical Mark IV. On the day we toured the *Cod,* one of our group was wildly excited to discover it was nearly identical to the one on which he'd served. Some 30 years and maybe 100 pounds after his tour of duty, Dick dove through hatches and navigated ladders like the 19-year-old bubblehead he used to be. Soon Dick was leading a large group of tourists through the spaces he'd known intimately. He showed off his torpedo room bunk, his cramped workspace, and the crew mess that could seat 24 if everyone kept their elbows tucked. Your tour might not be as personal, but you'll enjoy it just as much. The *Cod* is open May through September.

DUM DUM LOLLIPOPS, SPANGLER CANDY WORLD, BRYAN

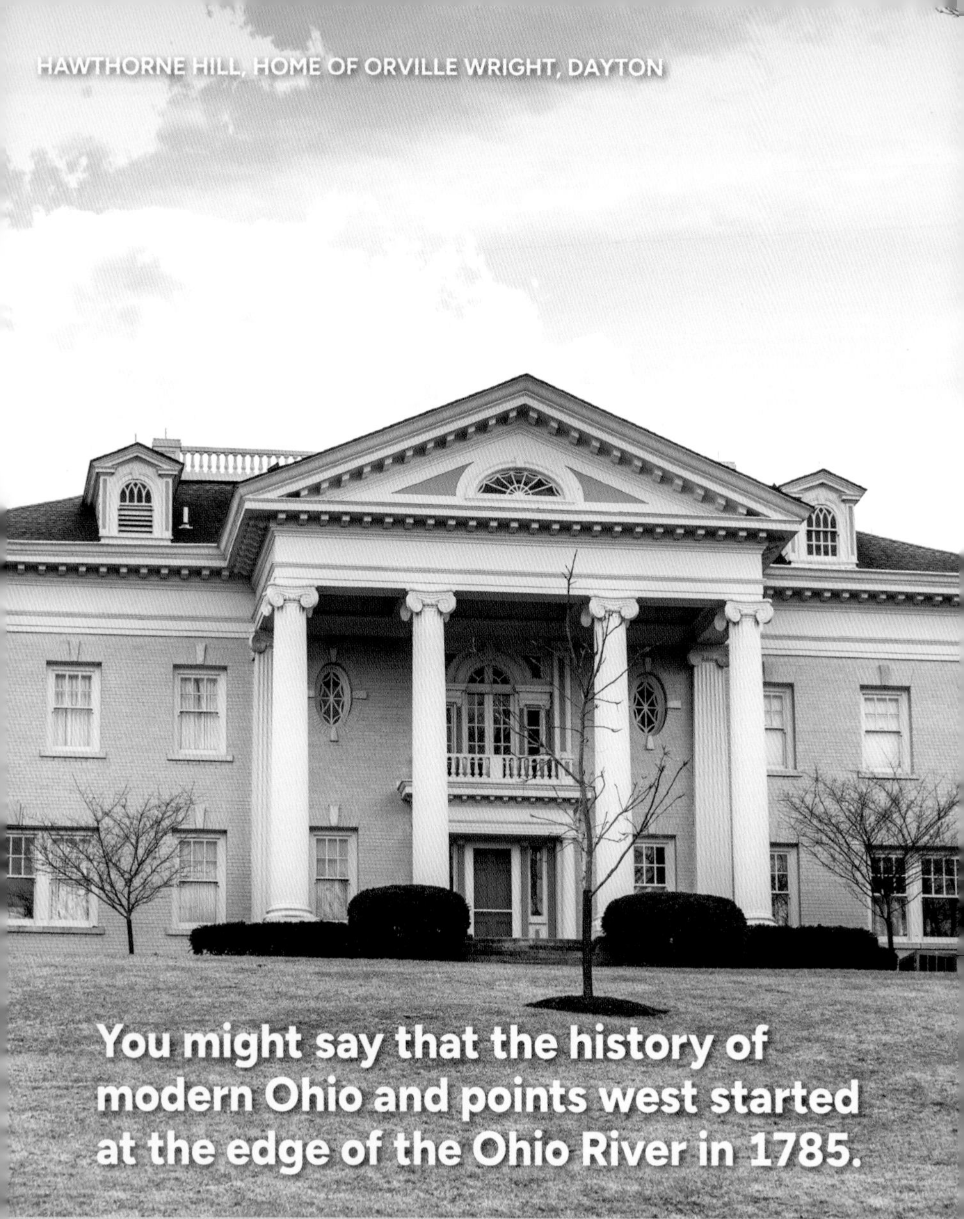

HAWTHORNE HILL, HOME OF ORVILLE WRIGHT, DAYTON

**You might say that the history of modern Ohio and points west started at the edge of the Ohio River in 1785.**

The survey point established by Thomas Hutchins (see Point of Beginning, page 136) opened the Northwest Territory. European settlers flocked to the Ohio country to trade with, live among, and eventually fight against local Native American tribes. This history is filled with tragedy, but also with exciting and notable achievements.

*Welcome to*

# OHIO HISTORY

## 209 DAYTON AVIATION HERITAGE NATIONAL HISTORICAL PARK ............ 133

**Dayton**

Orville and Wilbur Wright were busy people. They manufactured, sold, rented, and repaired bicycles; owned a printing business; were classmates of and publishers for author and poet Paul Laurence Dunbar—and oh, yes, they built airplanes in their spare time.

## 210 FORT MEIGS ........................ 133

**Perrysburg**

View a reenactment of the sieges that occurred here during the War of 1812. If just watching doesn't seem like enough excitement, you can sign up to participate.

## 211 HISTORIC FORT STEUBEN .................. 133

**Steubenville**

When you visit a place like Fort Steuben, you expect to learn about frontier history and people. You wouldn't necessarily expect to learn about entertainer Dean Martin too.

## 212 JOHN H. MORGAN SURRENDER SITE ............... 134

**West Point**

This Confederate general crossed the Ohio River against orders in 1863 and terrified the populace for two months. It didn't end well for him.

## 213 JOHNSON'S ISLAND CIVIL WAR MILITARY PRISON ............. 134

**Johnson's Island**

There's not much left of this prison site except for the cemetery. For insights into the sad consequences of war, though, drive over the causeway to pay your respects.

## 214 MAY 4 MEMORIAL & VISITORS CENTER .......... 134

**Kent**

Kent State University became the focal point of an unhappy nation in May 1970, when National Guardsmen killed four students during a protest against the Vietnam War.

## 215 MCCOOK HOUSE CIVIL WAR MUSEUM ......... 135

**Carrollton**

Another tiny intersection between Ohioans and the faraway Civil War is here, at the home of the Fighting McCooks.

## 216 THE OHIO CANAL SYSTEM ................... 135

**Statewide**

Before railroads and paved roads came along, freight traveled through Ohio via two north-south

**Of the eight presidents who were born and/or raised in Ohio, four died in office.**

canals and their feeders that stretched from Lake Erie to the Ohio River

**217 OHIO HISTORY CENTER** .............. 136

**Columbus**

Headquarters of the Ohio History Connection, this is the place to be for a comprehensive look at the legacy of the state.

**218 OHIO VILLAGE** ...................... 136

**Columbus**

This is a fun place to visit. You can talk to the "villagers" about their lives, take in a vintage "baseball" game, or climb aboard a high-wheeled bicycle.

**219 POINT OF BEGINNING** ....... 136

**East Liverpool**

Geographers worldwide are aware of this important surveyors' point, where the systematic land surveying of the Northwest Territory had its beginnings.

**220 ST. HELENA HERITAGE PARK** ................. 137

**Canal Fulton**

Ride the *St. Helena III* through an original section of the Ohio and Erie Canal.

*Find out more about*

# OHIO HISTORY

## 209 DAYTON AVIATION HERITAGE NATIONAL HISTORICAL PARK

**16 S. Williams Street, Dayton, OH 45402; 937-225-7705 nps.gov/daav**

This park has seven locations in Dayton that preserve the history of both Wilbur and Orville Wright and Paul Laurence Dunbar. At the **Huffman Prairie Interpretive Center and Flying Field,** visitors learn about the Wright brothers' invention of the first practical airplane and their flying school. The **Wright Memorial,** a granite obelisk, is nearby. The **Wright-Dunbar Interpretive Center** is on the location of the Wright and Wright Print Shop, and next door to the restored **Wright Cycle Shop.** From 1895 to 1897, the brothers operated a bicycle business here, using their profits to experiment with powered human flight. Interpretive exhibits and displays at the center include the **Parachute Museum.** At the **Paul Laurence Dunbar House** (see page 87), you can explore the legacy of the writer and poet. **Carillon Historical Park** (see page 5) is an open-air history museum and houses the original 1905 *Wright Flyer III*. Guided ranger tours are available at the two interpretive centers during summer months.

## 210 FORT MEIGS

**29100 West River Road, Perrysburg, OH 43551; 419-874-4121 fortmeigs.org**

Taking a simple hour-long tour of this War of 1812 fort won't be enough for the curious and imaginative. Fort Meigs offers a mind-boggling array of demonstrations, lectures, themed reenactments, workshops, hands-on crafts, holiday events, and just plain fun, for everyone from toddlers to grandpas and grandmas.

The reenactments include the First Siege on Memorial Day weekend, Muster on the Maumee over Father's Day weekend, the Independence Day reenactment in July, and the Garrison Ghost Walk on two weekends in October. The British and their allies attempted to storm the fort twice but were defeated both times. The visitor center is open Wednesday through Sunday year-round, but the fort itself is only open from April through October.

## 211 HISTORIC FORT STEUBEN

**120 South Third Street, Steubenville, OH 43952; 740-283-1787 oldfortsteuben.com**

A nicely reconstructed 1786 fort along the Ohio River offers visitors a unique look at early European settlers and their lives. Named for Baron von Steuben of Revolutionary War fame, the fort was founded by the First American Regiment to protect surveyors as the Northwest Territory was being developed. Beginning in 2024, a Museum of Surveying is to be constructed within the fort with the help of the University of Akron and the Professional Land Surveyors of Ohio. The original Federal Land Office for the area is also on the site. An exhibit hall features rotating exhibits about Native Americans, Colonial life, and Ohio and American history. Archaeological digs have been conducted by the Franciscan University of Steubenville at the fort since 1978, and there is an annual summer field school for students. Other yearly activities include Frontier Days and Constitution Week. The visitor center devotes a small section to Steubenville's most famous son, entertainer Dean Martin.

## 212 JOHN H. MORGAN SURRENDER SITE

**State Route 518,**
**0.2 mile east of County Road 784,**
**between Gavers and West Point, OH**
**GPS: 40.69805°, -80.74722°**
**advkeen.co/surrender_site**
**advkeen.co/morgans_surrender**

It's easy to miss, and you might have to turn around a time or two, but history buffs often search out this good-size boulder along Route 518 just to read the brass plaque commemorating the surrender site of wayward Confederate Brigadier General John Hunt Morgan. Morgan wanted to draw Union forces away from the southern battlefields, and for two months he succeeded, as he and more than 2,000 men crossed southern Ohio, ransacking as they went. He began on June 11, 1863, but was down to 475 men by mid-July, harassed and chased by Union troops. He made it to Columbiana County by late July, then was caught by Union troops and surrendered with 355 men. Besides the monument, a piece of the trunk of the tree under which he surrendered was saved for posterity and can be seen at Beaver Creek State Park near East Liverpool.

## 213 JOHNSON'S ISLAND CIVIL WAR MILITARY PRISON

**3510 Confederate Drive,**
**Johnson's Island, OH 43440**
**419-448-2327**
**johnsons-island.org**

Many of the 206 grave markers in this National Historic Landmark bear the same word: *unknown*. The United Daughters of the Confederacy erected the markers in the early 1900s, but identifying remains has been difficult. The graves were originally topped only with wooden crosses, and records from the time are sketchy. The federal government leased half the island from the Johnson family in 1861, and more than 10,000 Confederate officers, soldiers, and a few civilians were interned here during the Civil War. The complex covered 16 acres and held more than three dozen buildings. There were many escape attempts, especially when the lake was frozen, but only a few were successful. Heidelberg University has conducted archaeological digs on the island since 1989, and the Friends and Descendants of Johnson's Island Civil War Prison (FDJI) focus on preservation, education, and research efforts.

## 214 MAY 4 MEMORIAL & VISITORS CENTER

### 214A Library Archive

**1125 Risman Drive, Kent, OH 44243**
**330-672-3456**
**library.kent.edu/special-collections-and-archives/may-4-memorial-kent-state-university**

### 214B May 4 Visitors Center

**147 Taylor Hall,**
**300 Midway Drive,**
**Kent, OH, 44242**
**330-672-4660**
**kent.edu/may4**

There's not one good thing about visiting this memorial, but it almost seems a requirement. We need to remember what happened, even if we'll never fully understand why. On May 4, 1970, four students—two of whom were just on their way to class—were killed and nine wounded by National Guardsmen sent to quell student protests over US incursion into Cambodia during the Vietnam War. The memorial is a 2.5-acre wooded, flower-decked retreat for quiet reflection. The May 4 Visitors Center is located in Taylor Hall, near the site of the shootings. It follows the university's academic calendar, so it's closed during school breaks. Escorted walking tours are offered there, along with a documentary film. The KSU library on Risman Drive maintains a May 4 special collection. A commemorative event is held at KSU every May 4.

## 215 MCCOOK HOUSE CIVIL WAR MUSEUM

**15 South Lisbon Street,**
**Carrollton, OH 44615**
**330-627-3345 or 800-600-7172**
**advkeen.co/carroll_county**

The McCook homestead is a wonderfully imposing redbrick example of Federal architecture at the center of Carrollton. Daniel McCook, patriarch of the Fighting McCooks, enlisted in the Civil War at age 63. Eight sons and several nephews also enlisted. Daniel, while a major stationed at Cincinnati, was sent to capture Confederate General John Hunt Morgan during his invasion of Ohio but was killed by Morgan's troops near Buffington Island. (see John H. Morgan Monument, page 134).

McCook's sons Robert, Daniel, and Charles were also killed during the war, and Latimer, a battlefield surgeon, died in 1869 of disabilities resulting from the war. The McCook House has several authentically decorated rooms and a nice display of Civil War memorabilia. The house comes alive in November and December, with candlelight tours and a Festival of Trees.

## 216 THE OHIO CANAL SYSTEM

**Statewide**
**advkeen.co/canal_system**
**advkeen.co/canal_history**

In the early years of the 19th century, Ohioans made the expensive decision to connect their rivers and Lake Erie by human-made canals to carry farm products, freight, and passengers more easily. The first were the **Ohio & Erie Canal,** stretching from Cleveland to Portsmouth in the east, and the **Miami & Ohio Canal,** from Toledo to Cincinnati in the west. Feeders that connected to the Ohio & Erie were the **Pennsylvania & Ohio Canal,** the **Walhonding Canal,** the **Sandy & Beaver Canal,** the **Columbus Feeder,** and the **Hocking Canal.** Serving the Miami & Ohio were the **Wabash & Erie Canal,** the **Sidney Feeder,** and the **Cincinnati & Whitewater Canal.**

By the 1850s, railroads had begun to take business from the canals, but they continued to operate until heavy flooding in 1913 ended the canal era. Some interest revived in the 1960s, and portions of the old canals have been preserved. You can still take a canal boat ride on the Ohio & Erie aboard the *St. Helena III* (see St. Helena Heritage Park, page 137) in Canal Fulton and the *Monticello III* in Roscoe Village (see Roscoe Village, page 87). Parts of the Ohio & Erie can be seen in Cuyahoga Valley National Park. Along Route 66, segments of the Miami & Erie Canal still exist between Spencerville and Piqua. The Miami & Erie Canal Park is in West Carrollton. Traces of the Sandy & Beaver Canal are visible along OH 30 in Carrollton, and a few of its 90 locks, one of which is restored, are in Beaver Creek State Park. The remains of the Sidney Feeder can be seen from two hiking trails. The Hocking Canal, the longest of the feeders, has been paved over, but lock ruins can be seen near Haydenville and Nelsonville.

## 217 OHIO HISTORY CENTER

**800 East 17th Avenue,**
**Columbus, OH 43211**
**614-297-2300 or 800-686-6124**
**advkeen.co/history_center**

Immerse yourself in Ohio history here. Interactive exhibits start with the state's ancient beginnings and continue through westward expansion, war stories, battle flags, natural history and climate, endangered species, and the modern era. You can even learn about the Ohio-born White Castle hamburger chain. In short, the Ohio History Connection touches on nearly everything pertaining to Ohio. The museum is just the beginning, though. A genealogy research library is available here, as are resources for preserving historic homes and communities. Programs for teachers and students are offered. The campus is also home to Ohio Village (see below), the Ohio Village Muffins, and the Ohio Village Diamonds. The Muffins are male and the Diamonds are female, and both are vintage "baseball" teams that play, dress, and spell baseball by 1860s rules.

## 218 OHIO VILLAGE

**800 East 17th Avenue,**
**Columbus, OH 43211**
**614-297-2300 or 800-686-6124**
**advkeen.co/ohio_village**

This living-history museum in Columbus, part of the Ohio History Center, details the mid- to late-1800s in Ohio. There are 22 buildings, including some historic structures that were moved to the park. You won't be limited to looking at displays, though. Visitors are welcome to play with the toys, help with household chores, ride an adult tricycle around town, or browse period magazines. Town Hall, the Masonic Lodge, the Tinsmith Shop, the Ladies' Soldiers Aid Society, the Ohio Village Bank, and the Elk's Head Tavern are all places you can visit. The village's annual Halloween celebration includes a production of *The Legend of Sleepy Hollow*. The Ohio Cup Vintage Baseball Festival is also a popular annual event at the village, featuring the Ohio Village Muffins and the Lady Diamonds.

## 219 POINT OF BEGINNING

**State Route 39 at the Pennsylvania line,**
**East Liverpool, OH 43920**
**advkeen.co/liverpool_hist_society**
**advkeen.co/point_of_beginning**

A roadside obelisk in East Liverpool commemorates the beginning point of the U.S. Public Land Survey. The actual point is 1,112 feet to the south and now under the Ohio River. Geographer Thomas Hutchins drove a stake there September 30, 1785, along the north-south Ellicott's Line, and he used this point as the start of the east-west Geographer's Line. That stake marked the beginning of the rectangular land survey system and its initial surveyed tract, the 42-mile-wide Survey of the Seven Ranges. Surveying laid the groundwork for the wider settlement of Ohio by Europeans.

## 220 ST. HELENA HERITAGE PARK

**123 Tuscarawas Street Northwest, Canal Fulton, OH 44614**
**330-854-6835**
**advkeen.co/st-helena**

Part of the Ohio and Erie Canalway, this park covers 110 miles of the historic canal. It's an especially popular stop because of the *St. Helena III,* a canal boat replica you can ride. Horses pull the boat from a towpath alongside a section of the original canal. It's a leisurely and enjoyable way to spend an hour, riding gently along as a historian provides stories of the canal era and the surrounding countryside. Tours depart from the Canalway Center, and the boat can also be chartered. The Canalway Center offers interpretive information about the area and a 30-minute introductory video.

**Oberlin College, founded in 1833 in Oberlin, Ohio, was the first college to admit Black people and women, doing so from its very beginning.**

We're also famous for grapes, pumpkins, peaches, plums, pears, and berries. From mid-June, when the first strawberries are turning red, to late October, when there's frost on the pumpkins, pickers are covering the fields and orchards to gather in the harvest.

*Welcome to*

# ORCHARDS & VINEYARDS

**221**

### 221A A & M Farm Orchard
22141 State Route 251,
Midland, OH 45148
513-875-2500
advkeen.co/AM_farm_orchard

### 221B Apple Hill Orchards
1175 Lexington Ontario Road,
Mansfield, OH 44903
419-884-1500
Frederickstown orchard:
16908–16970 Upper
Frederickstown Amity Road,
Frederickstown, OH 43019
740-694-7688
applehillorchards.com

### 221C Beckwith Orchards
1617 Lake Rockwell Road,
Kent, OH 44240
330-673-6433
beckwithorchards.com

### 221D Branstool Orchards
5895 Johnstown-Utica Road
Northeast, Utica, OH 43080
740-892-3989
branstoolorchards.com

### 221E Burnham Orchards
8019 State Route 113,
Berlin Heights, OH 44814
419-588-2138
burnhamorchards.com

### 221F Cherry Orchards
10290 State Route 669 Northwest,
Crooksville, OH 43731
740-982-0976
advkeen.co/cherry_orchard

### 221G Conine's Country Market
20400 County Road 226,
Fostoria, OH 44830
419-435-9616 or 419-619-0031
coninescountrymarket.com

### 221H Fuhrmann Orchards
510 Hansgen Morgan Road,
Wheelersburg, OH 45694
740-776-6406

### 221I Hidden Hills Orchard
5680 State Route 26,
Marietta, OH 45750
740-376-9170
hiddenhillsorchard.com

### 221J Hillcrest Orchards
50336 Telegraph Road,
Amherst, OH 44001
440-965-8884
hillcrestfunfarm.com

### 221K Legend Hills Orchard & Country Store
11335 Reynolds Road,
Utica, OH 43080
740-892-2498
legendhillsorchard.com

### 221L MacQueen Orchards & Farm Market
7605 Garden Road,
Holland, OH 43528
419-865-2916
macqueenorchards.com

### 221M Miller Orchards
8690 Vermilion Road,
Amherst, OH 44001
440-988-8405
millerorchardsltd.com

**Ohio was once the largest wine producer in the country. Although wine production is lower today, the state still consistently puts out award-winning bottles.**

**221N The Orchard and Co.**
7255 N. London-Delaware Road,
Plain City, OH 43064
614-873-0510
theorchardandcompany.com

**221O Peace Valley Orchards**
5667 Adams Road,
Rogers, OH 44455
330-426-9695
pvoinc.com

**221P Peifer Orchards**
4590 US Highway 68 North,
Yellow Springs, OH 45387
937-767-2208
peiferorchards.com

**221Q Rittman Orchards**
13548 Mt. Eaton Road North,
Doylestown, OH 44230
330-925-4152
rittmanorchards.com

**221R Scenic Ridge Fruit Farms**
2031 State Route 89,
Jeromesville, OH 44840
419-368-3353
baumanorchards.com/locations
/scenic-ridge

**221S White House Fruit Farm**
9249 Youngstown Salem Road,
Canfield, OH 44406
330-533-4161
whitehousefruitfarm.com

CONCORD GRAPES RIPENING

UNDER THE CORE OF THE MILKY WAY AND THE DARK HORSE NEBULA AT JOHN GLENN ASTRONOMY PARK, HOCKING HILLS

**Ohioans believe they are at the heart of it all; that's especially true for outdoors adventure.**

From stargazing at John Glenn Astronomy Center to paddling the Muskingum River Water Trail, day-trippers have no lack of choices for adventure. Hiking at more than 70 state parks and sailing Lake Erie are also popular options. Whether you prefer the adrenaline rush of a zipline canopy tour in a state forest or a sedate wagon ride through The Wilds animal conservation center, Ohio has something for everyone.

# Welcome to OUTDOOR ADVENTURES

**All state parks are always free to everyone, unlike most other states that charge admission for at least some of their parks.**

## *Find out more about* OUTDOOR ADVENTURES

### 222 BUCKEYE TRAIL

**Statewide**
**Buckeye Trail Association, P.O. Box 5, Shawnee, OH 43782; 740-832-1282**
**buckeyetrail.org**

Hikers get a little of everything on the Buckeye Trail, and exercise is only part of the appeal. By following the trail's blue blazes, you can access remote areas of wilderness to view little-seen cliffs and waterfalls. At frequent intersections with history, hikers learn about Indian mounds, centuries-old forts, and restored canal locks. Though much of the trail is through woodland and along Forest Service trails, parts of it follow country roads and even sidewalks within city limits. The 26 trail sections are divided into roughly 50-mile segments and circumnavigate the state, from Cincinnati to Cleveland and back again. Yearly events include Morelfest and Biggest Day Hike.

### 223 CAESAR CREEK STATE PARK

**8570 East State Route 73, Waynesville, OH 45068-9719**
**513-897-3055**
**caesarcreekstatepark.com**

Caesar Creek was once visited only by hunters, Native Americans, and escaped slaves following the Underground Railroad. The creek valley was taken over by the U.S. Army Corps of Engineers in 1978 and became a state park that year. The park's active Nature Center Association maintains trails, hosts programs and presentations throughout the year, and assists with the park's annual Meteor Shower Campout. Hikers can visit Horseshoe Falls and Crawdad Falls and cross the Swinging Bridge on the 12.7-mile Perimeter Trail. Besides exploring 10 hiking trails, activities for visitors include archery, biking, camping, dog training, and swimming. A horse-friendly campground allows equestrians to take advantage of four bridle trails, ranging from 1.5 to 14 miles in length.

### 224 CLEVELAND VELODROME

**5033 Broadway Avenue (entrance off Pershing), Cleveland, OH 44127**
**clevelandvelodrome.org**

If you're a bicyclist, or even a potential bicyclist, you might check out this Olympic-style velodrome track. It's a bit more than 160 meters around and has a 50-degree embankment at the corners, reducing to 15 degrees on the straight sections. You must complete a class or be certified at another track in order to use the velodrome. Private sessions and coaching are available, or you can opt for open riding or an unlimited membership. If you want to race, you have to be approved by a track official. Sanctioned races are held some Friday and Saturday evenings. There's a comprehensive Youth Development Program. Sanctioned races and time trials are held throughout the season, and each year the velodrome hosts the Ohio State Championships. There is a women's weekend clinic every spring, and a NEOCycle Thunder Weekend festival every fall. The velodrome is open May through October.

## 225 CUYAHOGA VALLEY NATIONAL PARK

**6947 Riverview Road, Peninsula, OH 44264; 440-717-3890**
**nps.gov/cuva**

This national park stretches from Cleveland to Akron along the winding and scenic Cuyahoga River. Hiking and biking the Towpath Trail, where horses and mules once pulled barges, is a family-friendly activity since an excursion train, the Cuyahoga Valley Scenic Railroad (see page 5–6), runs along the same route. It's easy to hop on and off the train at different points along the trail, even if your family totes strollers, bicycles, tricycles, walkers, or wheelchairs. Sights to see include a reclaimed section of the Ohio and Erie Canal, CCC structures, a restored home, and wildlife that includes beavers, bald eagles, red and gray foxes, and herons.

## 226 GRAND LAKE ST. MARYS STATE PARK

**834 Edgewater Drive, St. Marys, OH 45885; 419-394-3611**
**ohiodnr.gov/go-and-do/plan-a-visit/find-a-property/grand-lake-st-marys-state-park**

Oil well derricks on a manmade Ohio lake? Believe it or not, Grand Lake St. Marys is famous for them. The first offshore oil drilling in the world took place here. Between 1891 and 1913, more than 100 oil well derricks dotted the lake. Since 1939, though, recreation has been the state park's primary mission on the 13,500-acre lake, which boasts 52 miles of shoreline. The family-friendly park offers cabins and a campground, unlimited horsepower boating, eight launch ramps, boat and slip rentals, four swimming beaches, ice fishing, all-access fishing, duck hunting, a nature center, two dog parks, trails, picnicking, and play areas.

Snowmobiling and cross-country skiing areas are available in wintertime. St. Marys Fish Hatchery on the eastern shore of the lake raises saugeye, walleye, yellow perch, channel catfish, and blue catfish to stock St. Marys and other local lakes.

## 227 MOHICAN STATE PARK

**3116 State Route 3, Loudonville, OH 44842**
**419-994-5125**
**ohiodnr.gov/go-and-do/plan-a-visit/find-a-property/mohican-state-park**

The Clear Fork of the Mohican River flows through this popular park and is the place to go in Ohio for river sports. On any summer weekend, convoys of floating, roped-together tubes are a common sight. There's one for mom, one for dad, more for each kid, another for the dog, and, of course, one for the picnic cooler. Colorful kayaks swish through gentle rapids while novices in rental canoes learn the basics on the user-friendly river. Hiking, bicycling, and bridle trails crisscross the park. A particularly challenging trail for mountain biking and hiking loops 24.5 miles around a gorge. The trail is regularly labeled one of the "best" and "must-ride" spots and is a stop on the National Ultra Endurance Series.

## 228 MOTORCYCLING

**Statewide**
**motorcycleroads.com/motorcycle-rides-in/ohio**

The Appalachian foothills of eastern and southern Ohio are the place to be for motorcyclists who crave curves and switchbacks. State Route 555, also known as the Triple Nickel, is a popular route, stretching from Little Hocking on the Ohio River northwest toward Roseville. The Black Diamond Run stitches together small towns around Wayne National Forest that were important to the area's coal heritage. State Route 170, beginning in East Liverpool and winding north to Poland, was named one of the top-10 motorcycle roads in the United States by *American Motorcyclist* magazine. The Dragon's Tail coils along Route 78 between McConnelsville and Glouster, up and down the hills and back and forth through the hairpin turns known as "the twisties." State Route 147 curves through what is known as Little Switzerland, an area famous for its hilltop vistas and Amish farms.

### RALLIES

#### 228A AMA Vintage Motorcycle Days, yearly in July

**Mid-Ohio Sports Car Course,**
**7721 Steam Corners Road,**
**Lexington, OH 44904; 800-262-5646**
**vintagemotorcycledays.com**

#### 228B Ohio Bike Week, around Memorial Day

**5316 Milan Road, Unit 2,**
**Sandusky, OH 44870; 419-502-0022**
**ohiobikeweek.com**

#### 228C Thunder on the Strip, around Labor Day

**Geneva-on-the-Lake, OH 44041**
**440-466-1768 or 440-466-2361**
**thunderonthestrip.com**

MOHICAN COVERED BRIDGE, LOUDONVILLE

## 229 MUSKINGUM RIVER WATER TRAIL

**Statewide**
**advkeen.co/muskingum_trail**

If you're in the mood for a scenic boat cruise and the old-fashioned appeal of hand-operated locks, head straight for the Muskingum River Water Trail, which is open to recreational traffic for 112 miles, from Dresden to Marietta. In the 1800s, the Muskingum River was improved with locks, dams, and side-cut canals to connect the Ohio and Erie Canal to the Ohio River. When commerce slowed to a halt after the Civil War, the river gradually returned to recreational use, after restoration work by the U.S. Army Corps of Engineers and the state of Ohio. In 2006, the lock system became the first Navigation Historic District in the United States. It's also a National Historic Civil Engineering Landmark. Besides canal and frontier history and artifacts, boaters can investigate Underground Railroad history, as the Muskingum was a busy corridor for escaped slaves before the Civil War.

## 230 MUSKINGUM WATERSHED CONSERVANCY DISTRICT

**1319 3rd Street Northwest,**
**New Philadelphia, OH 44663**
**877-363-8500**
**mwcd.org**

The 10 reservoirs of the district were created to prevent flooding and help native wildlife, but for sports enthusiasts, they mean premier fishing and boating opportunities, drawing large crowds of boaters and campers. But there's much more here. Do you like moonlight kayak tours? Fishing tournaments? Boat races? Beach parties? All of them are scheduled throughout the year. Eight of the lakes have campgrounds, and there are nine marinas among them. An equestrian camp and a trail system that connects to Malabar Farm State Park are available at Pleasant Hill Lake Park, and a state water trail is in the works. All of the parks have numerous hiking trails. Tappan Lake serves as regional headquarters for the Buckeye Trail Association.

## 231 OHIO POWER RECREATIONAL AREAS

**southeast Ohio; 740-962-1205**
**aep.com/recreation/areas**

What does a power company do with strip mining areas when all the coal is gone? American Electric Power built lakes and trails. The **Conesville Coal Lands** have more than 10,000 acres available for public hunting and fishing near **Coshocton,** plus an equine trail area. Camping is available for horse owners only, with a three-day limit. The **Poston Post Lands** near Athens include 1,760 acres for hunters only. Two more hunting-and-fishing zones are the **Southern Ohio Recreation Area** near Athens, with more than 4,000 acres; and **Fairbanks Landing** near Rutland, with 8,000 acres for public hunting and fishing. The Wilds (see page 150) is also part of the Ohio Power Recreational Areas.

## 232 OHIO TO ERIE TRAIL

**Statewide**
**614-918-3636**
**ohiotoerietrail.org**

If you're a bicyclist but don't always want to travel on public roads, check out the Ohio to Erie Trail, which primarily follows railroad and canal routes. Besides bicyclists, the trail wel-

EGG-SHAPED TUNNEL ALONG THE OHIO TO ERIE TRAIL, STATEWIDE

comes hikers, wheelchair users, rollerbladers, and equestrians. The trail crosses the state diagonally, connecting Cleveland, Akron, Columbus, and Cincinnati. Twenty-two regional sections make up the 326 miles of the route. The OTET awards membership in their 326 Club to those who complete the trail on consecutive days in segments within a calendar year.

## 233 PYMATUNING STATE PARK

**6100 Pymatuning Lake Road, Andover, OH 44003; 440-293-6030**
**ohiodnr.gov/go-and-do/plan-a-visit/find-a-property/pymatuning-state-park**

One of the running jokes around campfires at Pymatuning is whether Ohio fish taste better than Pennsylvania fish. It's a legitimate question, since the 14,000-acre reservoir and surrounding park straddle the state line. Walleye and muskellunge are the ones to catch, and Ohio fish definitely taste better, whether you snag them from the deck of your pontoon, through the ice, or from the shore at your campsite. Besides boating, fishing, and swimming, visitors can trap or hunt (with firearms and bows) during the fall and winter. Campers can choose from some 350 sites on the Ohio side, or more than 50 cabins. Nesting bald eagles have made a home at one end of the Ohio-side campground for several years, and they are best viewed from the water. Sharp-eyed birders can also spot great blue herons and red-tailed hawks.

## 234 WAYNE NATIONAL FOREST

**13700 US Highway 33, Nelsonville, OH 45764; 740-753-0101**
**fs.usda.gov/wayne**

Wildflowers and forest songbirds populate Wayne National Forest, along with plenty of native animals. You might not actually see a bobcat on the 15-mile loop in Wildcat Hollow, but be on the lookout for wild turkeys and salamanders. Outdoor enthusiasts flock to the 250,000 acres of Wayne National Forest, not just to enjoy nature, but for camping, horseback and off-highway vehicle riding, and hunting. Rock climbing and rappelling are allowed in the forest, but not encouraged. Big Bend Swimming Beach is available on Lake Vesuvius. Nine different campgrounds are scattered throughout the forest; some are walk-in only, while others offer RV sites for a reasonable fee. Both big- and small-game hunting is allowed in sections of the forest away from camping, day-use, and mining areas. Wayne National Forest may be renamed Buckeye National Forest because of requests from Native Americans and from local communities.

## 235 THE WILDS

**14000 International Road,
Cumberland, OH 43732
740-638-5030
thewilds.org**

Picture this: The sun sets over a ridgeline in the distance as you amble on horseback through wildflowers that are alive with butterflies seeking a last meal before dark. To your left is a lumbering herd of white rhinos that includes a calf. In the middle distance, two giraffes sway across the track. Tonight, you'll stay at Nomad Ridge, enjoying a catered dinner at your campfire before retiring to your private yurt. After a catered breakfast, you'll visit a conservation center dedicated to the endangered eastern hellbender salamander. Are you deep in the heart of Africa? India? China? No, you're in Cumberland, Ohio, visiting The Wilds, which is one of the largest conservation centers in the world. Species represented on the 10,000-acre property include Bactrian camels, ostriches, cheetahs, takins, and oryx. Horseback and bus tours are available, as are a variety of camps and group events. Don't miss the aeolian harp near the visitor center.

GREATER ONE-HORNED ASIAN RHINO, THE WILDS, CUMBERLAND

## 236 ZIPLINE, CANOPY, & CLIMBING/ RAPPELLING TOURS

Statewide

Adrenaline junkies should head to southern Ohio for 50-mph zipline tours. Once a thrill-seeker is strapped into a harness, an overhead cable sends them zooming hundreds of feet through treetops and across rivers and lakes. Slightly less-adventurous folks can opt for canopy tours that feature elevated walkways and bridges through treetops. Some companies offer "kid-friendly" ziplines for children as young as 5. Additional options include moonlight zip tours and canopy walks, ground-level Segway excursions, and add-on trips to nearby attractions. Climbing and rappelling adventures are a little harder to find, but once you get there, great fun is in store.

### 236A Adventure Rock Climb & Rappel Hocking Hills Adventure Trek

Logan, OH 43138; 740-777-2579
hockinghillsadventuretrek.com

### 236B Akron Fossils & Science Center Ziplining

2080 South Cleveland-Massillon Road, Copley, OH 44321; 330-665-3466
akronfossils.org/zip-line

### 236C Common Ground Canopy Tours

14240 Baird Road,
Oberlin, OH 44074; 440-707-2044
commongroundcenter.org

### 236D High Rock Adventures

10108 Opossum Hollow Road,
Rockbridge, OH 43149; 740-385-9886
advkeen.co/hocking_climbing

### 236E Hocking Hills Canopy Tours

10714 Jackson Street,
Rockbridge, OH 43149; 740-385-9477
hockinghillscanopytours.com

### 236F Holden Arboretum

9550 Sperry Road,
Kirtland, OH 44094; 440-602-3838
holdenfg.org/attractions/holden-arboretum/kalberer-emergent-tower

### 236G Toledo Zoo & Aquarium Ziplining

2 Hippo Way, Toledo, OH 43609
419-385-5721
toledozoo.org/adventure-course

### 236H Valley Zipline Tours

3465 Duffy Road Southeast,
Lancaster, OH 43130; 740-654-3392
valleyziplinetours.com

### 236I Wild Zipline Safari

14000 International Road,
Cumberland, OH 43732
740-638-5030
thewilds.org/zipline-safari

HOLDEN ARBORETUM CANOPY WALK, KIRTLAND

TO SOME, THIS IS JUST AN AGING WALL; TO OTHERS, IT IS A PERFECT CANVAS.

**There's something about a blank wall that makes an artist want to decorate it—or at least advertise on it.**

When I was a child, a blank wall overlooking Dresden Avenue in my hometown advertised Uneeda Biscuits. These days, artists are more likely to celebrate town history and the evolution of art than biscuits.

# Welcome to OUTDOOR MURALS

*Find out more about*

# OUTDOOR MURALS

## 237 DAYTON MURALS

**Dayton, OH**
**advkeen.co/mural_guide2**
**advkeen.co/murals_guide**
**advkeen.co/short_north_arts_district**

There's no handy, collated brochure listing all of the Dayton murals, but you can download an app for a self-guided tour (see third website above). Or you may want to search them out for yourself. Some are whimsical, like the birds on a railroad bridge at Keowee and First Streets. Several celebrate music, at least two are commemorative, and others are just fun and full of color. A favorite of mine is the cats mural that decorates a bistro on East Fifth Street in the Oregon District. Besides pleasing the eye, it serves as a fundraiser for local animal-welfare groups. Another favorite behind a café on Brown Street is a 6-foot stack of pancakes accompanied by a short stack of cupcakes. On North Jefferson Street there's a bright-and-flashy collage of doves based on a Paul Laurence Dunbar poem. A more-somber mural on East Third Street honors Dayton native and astronaut Charles Bassett II, who was killed in a jet crash. Another commemorative mural fills a retaining wall on Keowee Street between First and Third Streets. The mural, called *Love You* remembers people who have died by suicide.

## 238 FRANKLIN MURALS

**Franklin, OH 45005; 937-746-8457**
**advkeen.co/franklin_murals**
**advkeen.co/franklin_attractions**

The amazing thing about the Franklin murals, painted by award-winning muralist and Ohio native Eric Henn, is their perspective. At first sight, you almost think you can go into that diner for an ice-cream cone; cross the bridge between the lions; or walk across actual grass, under actual stone arches, and into the painted Victorian park. The veterans' mural on the side of VFW Post 7596, at first glance, really does look like a sculpture. The transportation mural covers everything: horses, buggies, canals, steamships, railways, biplanes, and cars.

## 239 PORTSMOUTH FLOODWALL MURALS

**Portsmouth, OH 45662**
**portsmouthohiomurals.com**

It took nine years for Robert Dafford and his local assistants to paint the original set of murals here. Since then, more have been added. The nearly ¾ mile of murals is thought to be the largest assemblage painted by a single artist. Starting at the east end, the murals are chronological, beginning with the depiction of a local Hopewell mound complex. The murals progress through history, celebrating frontier notables like Shawnee leader Tecumseh and town surveyor Henry Massie. Olympic athlete Jim Thorpe, baseball legend Branch Rickey, and actor Roy Rogers are memorialized. One section depicts the 1937 flood, which was the catalyst for the floodwall itself. Steamships, farm scenes, canals, cityscapes, industry, and scenic vistas are included. Don't expect to take it all in at once, just enjoy it one mural at a time.

## 240 SHORT NORTH ARTS DISTRICT

**21 East 5th Avenue, Suite 103, Columbus, OH 43201**
**614-299-8050**
**advkeen.co/short_north_arts_district**

Many of the permanent murals in this arts district between The Ohio State University and downtown Columbus are, well, interpretive. Picture the farmer's daughter from Woods' *American Gothic* upside down. Or consider the meaning of *Mona Lisa* on her side. Or contemplate *Life Force,* which depicts a man with a sunflower for a head. Even the electrical utility cabinets on the sidewalks of Short North have been enlivened with art from emerging artists. The Short North Alliance hosts Summer Spray, which commissions artists for a live mural-painting event. The artists succeed each other over several weeks to showcase unity and diversity.

## 241 STEUBENVILLE MURALS

**Steubenville Visitor Center, 120 South Third Street, Steubenville, OH 43952**
**866-301-1787**
**visitsteubenville.com/what-to-do /steubenville-murals**

*The Ladies of the Seminary* on Market Street is possibly the most thought-provoking mural in downtown Steubenville. Staring up at it, you have to wonder: Is it a coincidence that they all have the same hairstyle? Could that woman on the upper left be asleep? Did they like going to a school for young ladies, or did they hate it? All of the 25 murals make you stop and think about the way things worked in bygone days. Everything from the High Shaft Mine to a boy's first bank deposit is memorialized, depicting everyday life in an Ohio River town. There's even a mural dedicated to favorite son Dean Martin. You can walk to all but two of the murals, which are 1.5 miles from town in Holly-wood Plaza. The Steubenville Visitor Center, located on the grounds of Historic Fort Steuben (see page 133–134), offers a brochure with mural locations. Guided tours can also be arranged there.

## 242 WELLSVILLE FLOODWALL MURALS

**Lisbon Street, Wellsville, OH 43968**
**330-532-2120**
**waymarking.com/waymarks /WM5CVF_Village_Flood _Wall Wellsville_Ohio**

Local artist Gina Hampson is responsible for painting and maintaining the murals on Wellsville's flood wall. Each mural is set as a view through a window, and Hampson surrounded each window with thousands of painted red bricks that you could swear are real. The flood wall isn't in the most picturesque location, running under a bridge along Yellow Creek, but the town's revitalization committee has made the area inviting, with lighting, a sidewalk, and landscaping. The murals fill both sides of the wall and include depictions of the city's notable buildings, its pottery heritage, and the long-vanished outcrop that resembles a Native American's head. Some historic events are also included, notably Abraham Lincoln's visit to Wellsville a month before his assassination.

## 243 YELLOW SPRINGS MURALS

**Keith's Alley and Xenia Avenue,**
**Yellow Springs, OH 45387**
**advkeen.co/yellowpedia_murals**

The murals here, which you have to seek out on your own, represent many styles, from the historical to the abstract. There's even a modern version of cave art, featuring sprinting buffalo. The bicycle mural is a compelling minimalist sketch. Two recent murals, one outside and one inside, decorate the artist's favorite pizza shop. Another pair, in Keith's Alley, commemorate George Floyd.

A VIBRANT GEOMETRIC MURAL, TOLEDO

ROCK HOUSE, LOGAN

**If you're interested in geology and fossils, or think you might be, these day trips should make your bucket list.**

From glittering calcium carbonate to the more humble coal and flint, Ohio has a lot to show visitors.

## *Welcome to* ROCKS & MINERALS

**Ohio is rich in fossils and is known for key specimens of *Dunkleosteus terrelli,* a fish from the Devonian period thought to be up to 29 feet long and four metric tons.**

**254 TRAMMEL FOSSIL PARK** ........................ 163

**Sharonville**

Bring the kids along, and some digging tools, for a great day of fossil-hunting.

FLINT IS THE OFFICIAL GEMSTONE OF OHIO. THIS IS A FLINT-KNAPPED ARROWHEAD FROM THE PENNSYLVANIAN OF OHIO, COSHOCTON

## *Find out more about* ROCKS & MINERALS

### 244 AKRON FOSSILS & SCIENCE CENTER

**2080 South Cleveland Massillon Road, Copley, OH 44321; 330-665-3466**
**akronfossils.org**

It's all about fun here—hands-on, educational, and sometimes messy fun. The focus is not on learning science, but on experiencing it. Guided tours are only the start of an impressive array of programming that includes Super Science Saturdays, summer camps, and K-12 programs. There are also annual adventure trips like canoeing Minnesota's Boundary Waters. Don't miss the Creation Museum, which explores the origin of the universe. Outside, Play Park is a 2-acre space with a 200-foot zipline, a 60-foot slide, and a mini challenge course.

### 245 CRYSTAL CAVE

**978 Catawba Avenue, Put-In-Bay, OH 43456; 419-285-2811**
**advkeen.co/heinemans_winery**
**advkeen.co/crystal_cave**

Gustav Heineman was just trying to dig a well for his winery in 1887, but instead he found the world's largest celestine geode. It was a small limestone cave to begin with, lined with a bluish mineral called celestine, a form of strontium sulfate. Originally, Heineman allowed mining of the celestite, which was used to make fireworks. That made the cave much bigger, and it turned out to be a good thing for Heineman. Just in time for Prohibition, when he had to stop making wine, he discovered that allowing tourists into the cave was a great way to make money. Tours are still a good source of revenue at the winery and are offered May through September.

### 246 FLINT RIDGE ANCIENT QUARRIES & NATURE PRESERVE

**15300 Flint Ridge Road, Glenford, OH 43739; 740-763-4127**
**advkeen.co/flint_ridge_quarries**
**advkeen.co/flint_ridge**

What has been called the "Great Indian Quarry of Ohio" doesn't look all that impressive when you drive in, but when you consider the site's overwhelming importance in the daily lives of Ohio's first human inhabitants, you start to develop a little respect. Flint Ridge has almost 8 miles of high-quality flint, 2 to 10 feet thick, in a dizzying array of colors. Besides plain old gray and white, there's pink, yellow, blue, green, black, and copper-colored flint as well. People of the Hopewell culture excavated hundreds of quarry pits to mine flint that they knapped (worked) into tools and weapons. Flint made it easy for them to hunt, butcher meat, harvest plants, make clothing, construct shelters, and defend themselves. The preserve includes a museum filled with Native American artifacts and natural curiosities, like trilobites. There are several walking trails that skirt the quarry pits, which are now filled with water.

### 247 HISTORY OF COAL MUSEUM

**200 East Market Street, Cadiz, OH 43907; 740-942-2623**
**thecoalmuseum.com**

Underground and surface coal mining have a long and sometimes brutal history in Ohio. A history of the industry is chronicled at this museum in the lower level of the Puskarich Public Library. Displays include tools and equipment, watch fobs, company store scrip (currency), lunch buckets, and clothing. Safety equipment on display ranges from a canary cage to self-contained rescue kits. There are coal cars, pieces of equipment, and a model of a surface mine operation. Many photographs are available, some showing smiling miners in clean clothes, and others showing exhausted, beaten-down workers after an underground shift. One chilling part of the collection is the archive of stories dedicated to mining disasters. Newspaper accounts of 19th-century incidents spare no details. One account reports, "The man who caused the explosion was badly mutilated. His body was burned to a crisp."

## 248 KARL E. LIMPER GEOLOGY MUSEUM

**Miami University,**
**126 Shideler Hall, Oxford, OH 45056**
**513-529-3220**
**miamioh.edu/cas/academics/centers/limper-museum**

You might not think rocks and minerals are that exciting, but the glittering displays in this museum are fascinating. The building houses specimens of rocks, minerals, and fossils from around the world, not to mention meteorites. The museum is meant to educate students and interested visitors on basic geology, especially that of the local area. Groups of 30 or less are welcome with advance notice. Groups of more than 30 can split and rotate among the geology museum, an herbarium, and a natural-history museum on the campus.

## 249 MINERS' MEMORIAL PARK

**4470 State Route 78 East,**
**McConnelsville, OH 43756**
**740-453-4377**
**advkeen.co/miners_memorial**
**advkeen.co/Big_muskie_bucket**

The centerpiece of this small picnic area in Jesse Owens State Park is the Big Muskie Bucket. How big is it? Let's just say you could almost fit two cars in it. The bucket is all that's left of the Big Muskie dragline excavator, which strip-mined coal in southeast Ohio between 1969 and 1991. Big Muskie was the largest single-bucket dragline ever built, costing $25 million in 1969. It could lift 325 tons at a scoop. Working around the clock, it moved more than 400 million cubic yards of earth and rock in its 22 years of operation.

The park also includes information on the history of the Central Ohio Coal Company, as well as a Wall of Honor listing the company's employees.

## 250 OAKES QUARRY PARK

**1267 East Xenia Drive,**
**Fairborn, OH 45324;**
**937-754-3090**
**advkeen.co/oakes_quarry**
**drydredgers.org/oakes_quarry.htm**

Limestone was surface-quarried here in the 1920s, and the quarry was privately owned until the Oakes family donated it to Fairborn in 2003. Trails through the park for hikers and horseback riders lead through deposits of limestone fossils left by mining activity. The Silurian Age crinoid fossils are said to be the best in the United States. Personal collecting is only allowed from a designated pile, which is marked by a sign. The park encompasses 190 acres and has two miles of hiking and horseback trails, plus portable restrooms.

## 251 OHIO CAVERNS

**2210 East State Route 245, West Liberty, OH 43357; 937-465-4017 ohiocaverns.com**

This is a fracture cave, which means that, in some places, especially on the Historic Tour, you'll wiggle and twist and hoist yourself through tight passageways and steep climbs. The Limestone Tour, though, is wheelchair accessible. For those able, I recommend combining the Historic Tour with the Natural Wonder Tour. There is also a Winter Tour, which is all that is offered October through April. The caverns are home to some rare and ethereal dual formations, as well as soda straws, cave bacon, and the largest stalactite in Ohio. The caverns are set in a pretty 35-acre park that has two pavilions for rent, a picnic area, playground, restrooms, gift shop, and a gem-mining sluice. Bags of mining materials can be purchased in the gift shop, and other supplies are provided.

## 252 ROCKBRIDGE STATE NATURE PRESERVE

**11475 Dalton Road, Rockbridge, OH 43149; 614-265-6561 ohiodnr.gov/go-and-do/plan-a-visit/find-a-property/rockbridge-state-nature-preserve**

Home to a 100-foot natural bridge, this preserve is pretty basic, with no restrooms and no pets allowed. From the parking lot, it's a bit of a hike to the bridge, some of it alongside a steep drop-off. The main trail is 1.75 miles. A shorter 1-mile trail in the preserve leads to smaller rock formations. Getting to see the 100-foot natural bridge is worth the hike, though, as long as you have some good insect repellent. It was originally the ceiling of that recess cave next door, but most of it collapsed at some point, leaving the bridge. It's possible to walk (carefully!) across the top of the bridge, which is 10 to 20 feet wide.

## 253 ROCK HOUSE

**Hocking Hills State Park, 19852 State Route 664, Logan, OH 43138; 740-385-6842 ohiodnr.gov/go-and-do/plan-a-visit/find-a-property/hocking-hills-state-park**

This is not your ordinary state park hike. Hocking Hills visitors love to follow the trail out to Rock House, a wide 200-foot-long corridor carved from rock, halfway up a 150-foot sandstone cliff. But don't worry, you don't have to climb the cliff. There's a footbridge. The trail is rugged and includes some steps. Natural columns support the roof, and there are windows and niches along the sides. From the west side of the cave, you can look through a natural window to a waterfall. Native Americans used Rock House for shelter, as did some later unsavory types who earned the location the nickname Robbers' Roost.

## 254 TRAMMEL FOSSIL PARK

**11935 Tramway Drive, Sharonville, OH 45241; 513-563-2895 advkeen.co/trammel_park_guide advkeen.co/trammel_fossil**

The Trammel family donated 10 acres for this park after rare edrioasteroid fossils—echinoderms that are relatives of sea stars, sea urchins, and other marine animals—were found there. A pavilion at the park is built in the shape of the edrioasteroid. What makes the area such a great place for fossils is the layer of upper Ordovician limestone and shale. Helpful signage around the park explains the different formations and likely fossils to be found there. Visitors are welcome to dig for fossils and keep any that they find. If you go, wear shoes that are good for climbing, and don't forget your sunscreen.

THE GREAT LAKES SCIENCE CENTER AND HARBOR WALKWAY, CLEVELAND

## Ohio's many science museums and nature centers provide both recreation and inspiration.

Innovation, science, math, botany, zoology, and geology are just some of the topics covered in the displays and programs at these museums and centers. Age doesn't matter; everyone can enjoy a day strolling through a forest or trying hands-on activities.

# Welcome to SCIENCE MUSEUMS & NATURE CENTERS



**Dayton**

Discovery Zoo at the Boonshoft is the place to be for kids who are crazy about animals. Here, they can spend a day as a junior zookeeper or get a behind-the-scenes tour to feed and interact with the animals.



**Columbus**

What's not to love about COSI? It's not only a science and industry center, it's a place to laugh and play, marvel, and have a lot of fun.



**Milford**

This Cincinnati-area nature center is home to two separate nature sites, with more than 1,640 acres between them, as well as 20 miles of hiking trails.



**Cleveland**

Science centers tend to be heavily focused on education, but this one takes it a step further. MC2 STEM High School is located here.



**Toledo**

At this very hands-on science center, kids visiting the IDEA Lab are invited to tinker with balance experiments, computer programming, toys, musical instruments, and even trash bags.



**Logan**

When you tip up your head on a starry summer night, do you know what you're looking at? If not, astronomers at this park can teach you.



**Bay Village**

This science center focuses on wildlife, with live exhibits and rehabilitation services. The center's education programs include live animals that can sometimes be seen up close and hands-on.



**Willoughby Hills**

For a laid-back outdoors experience, you can't beat this nature center, set between Sanctuary Marsh and Sunset Pond.

## *Find out more about* SCIENCE MUSEUMS & NATURE CENTERS

### 255 BOONSHOFT MUSEUM OF DISCOVERY

**2600 DeWeese Parkway, Dayton, OH 45414; 937-275-7431**
**boonshoft.org**

Committed to hands-on science and zoology, the Boonshoft makes it easy for visitors to learn to appreciate everything from common subjects, such as our water supply, plus more exotic subjects, such as mole rats and other wildlife. A treehouse that extends beyond the walls of the museum provides opportunities to learn about environmental preservation. Watch a dinosaur skeleton being reassembled at the Paleo Lab, or discover the Bieser Room of Wonders. Conduct experiments in the Do Lab, or visit the astronomy collection to see a replica of Galileo's telescope. Then just for fun, stop at the White Allen Racetrack to see which cars and balls can zoom fastest along the double track. Summer STEM camps are held for children ages 5–14.

### 256 CENTER OF SCIENCE & INDUSTRY (COSI)

**333 West Broad Street, Columbus, OH 43215; 614-228-2674**
**cosi.org**

Since 1964, COSI has been the Ohio mecca for families and student groups. Even very young children have a great time here. At little kidspace, toddlers can climb, slide, build, and splash while they pretend to be fish, farmers, or engineers. Older children can explore the world of color and light, with all its meanings and possibilities. They can go to Big Science Park to lift a car with air power or discover nature. At other exhibits they can drive a Mars rover, hold a meteorite, and drive a unicycle through the air. For adults, COSI After Dark provides themed activities and games with adult beverages. COSI also boasts a National Geographic Giant Screen Theater with 3D technology and 4K projection. Its 60-foot planetarium offers live shows as well as several programs. The Atomic Café has a full menu, and at Molecules Brews and Bites you'll find snacks, hot and cold drinks, and beer and wine.

### 257 CINCINNATI NATURE CENTER

**Rowe Woods:**
**4949 Tealtown Road, Milford, OH 45150; 513-831-1711**
**Long Branch Farm and Trails:**
**6926 Gaynor Road, Goshen, OH 45122**
**513-831-1711**
**cincynature.org**

Visitors to these large-and-busy nature centers have two choices. The **Rowe Woods** location in Milford, open to members or via admission fees ($9 adults/$4 for kids 4–12, free for kids 3 and under), has 1,000 acres and more than 16 miles of hiking trails. **Long Branch Farm and Trails** in Goshen is accessible only to members and boasts 642 acres of deciduous forest, fields, streams, and ponds, plus 4 miles of hiking trails. The Cincinnati Nature Center was founded in 1965 with a vision to help the children of Cincinnati appreciate and understand the natural world. To that end, the center hosts a variety of children's programs, such as Homeschool Day, Cincy Nature Camp, Spring Break Camp, a Froggy Spotting Adventure stroll, a Family Nature Adventure camp, a Nature Preschool for little ones, Bug Hunts, as well as a Nature PlayScape. Children's parties are also popular at the center. For adults and families, there are bird, wildflower, and pond walks, as well as gardening and photography programs, organized hikes, and outdoor yoga. The center also offers a four-day Certified Interpretive Guide Course for people who aspire to work at a nature center or museum. Whatever your outdoor interest, you can probably find an event or class for it at the Cincinnati Nature Center.

## 258 GREAT LAKES SCIENCE CENTER

**601 Erieside Avenue,**
**Cleveland, OH 44114; 216-694-2000**
**greatscience.com**

Great Lakes Science Center's masterful set of guiding principles have made it a leader among science centers. They believe strongly in STEM education, critical and innovative thinking, and learning through curiosity and experimentation. To that end, the Center houses MC2 STEM High School, which encourages innovative learning for future scientists, engineers, and mathematicians. Exhibits at the Center follow the same principles, starting with the NASA Glenn Visitor Center. Interactive exhibits deal with living in space, exploration, and science and engineering principles in space. A six-story dome theater surrounds visitors with massive images and sound. The steamship *William G. Mather,* a restored Great Lakes freighter, is open for tours May through October.

## 259 IMAGINATION STATION

**1 Discovery Way, Toledo, OH 43604**
**419-244-2674**
**imaginationstationtoledo.org**

Family Think Tank Workshops and Family Explorer Clubs involve all ages at Imagination Station. Classes help families make discoveries and explore the world of physics to make their own fun. In the Just Tinkering program, anyone can turn a straw into a musical instrument, build windchimes, paint with light, craft an electronic greeting card, or build a cardboard pinball machine. Little ones can learn about shapes and colors as they crawl through the tunnels of the Baby Space. Older kids can learn encryption, build a hoop glider, or construct their own lava lamps. For adults, there are Downtown Movie Nights and periodic Science After Dark programs. The Station also hosts homeschool workshops, Scout programs, and summer camps.

## 260 JOHN GLENN ASTRONOMY PARK

**20294 State Route 664,**
**Logan, OH 43138; 877-403-4477**
**GPS: 39.433226°, -82.55412°**
**jgap.info**

Developed by Friends of the Hocking Hills State Park, this site was built to be as free of light pollution as possible. The plaza at the site was designed with ancient astrological calendars like Stonehenge and the Fort Ancient Earthworks in mind. Sunlight falls directly on the same spot in the plaza on the first day of each season.

Visitors are welcome anytime, whether programs are scheduled or not. During the weekend programs held March through November, stargazers can bring chairs, blankets, telescopes, cameras, and well-behaved pets on leashes. Programs start at sundown whenever the sky is clear, and it's prudent to get a parking pass from the website in advance, since parking is limited. If you've always wanted to learn more about our nighttime skies, you'll have a chance here to learn about stars, nebulae, constellations, planets, moons, comets, and galaxies. (See also The John and Annie Glenn Museum, page 109–110.)

## 261 LAKE ERIE NATURE & SCIENCE CENTER

**28728 Wolf Road,**
**Bay Village, OH 44140; 440-871-2900**
**lensc.org**

By becoming a Wild Pal, you can provide food, medication, and maintenance for a native animal at this center. Choices include raptors, snakes, turtles, skunks, and even a cute little tick-eating opossum. Wildlife education and conservation are focused on here. Programs are available for each age group, as well as for educators. The center boasts an active rehabilitation program that takes in more than 1,400 wild animals a year from 100 different species, returning critters to the wild as often as possible. The Walter R. Schuele Planetarium at the center offers Twinkle Tots for little ones and Sky-Quest for older visitors. There are also Telescope Nights, star parties, and workshops. Rental space and special programs are available for groups and parties.

## 262 NORTH CHAGRIN NATURE CENTER

**401 Buttermilk Falls Parkway,**
**Mayfield Village, OH 44094**
**440-473-3370**
**advkeen.co/north_chagrin**

This 1,700-acre wildlife sanctuary, part of the Cleveland Metroparks organization, offers a full schedule of activities for fans of the outdoors. The flat, paved trails at the center take you to an owl aviary, outdoor play areas and exhibits, and restful views of Sunset Pond and Sanctuary Marsh. There are regular birding programs, storytelling nights, and wildflower walks. Sunset Pond offers a prime viewing area for birds, mink, muskrats, and beaver. The deck of the Nature Center overlooks Sanctuary Marsh, which was developed in 1984. The deck is a good place to view ducks and geese. Inside the Nature Center is a play space for children, wildlife exhibits, and an auditorium. There's a bird-viewing area and aquariums for fish, reptiles, and amphibians. When you visit the center, save time for Squire's Castle. It's actually an 1890s gatehouse, but it looks like a medieval stone castle, complete with towers, turrets, and a portico. It's a popular local spot for weddings and photos.

EXPLORING LAKE ERIE NATURE & SCIENCE CENTER, BAY VILLAGE

PACKED STANDS FOR A FOOTBALL GAME

**Ohio is the proud home of two Major League Baseball clubs: the historic Cincinnati Reds (baseball's oldest club) and the Cleveland Guardians.**

And with the Cleveland Browns, the Cincinnati Bengals, and the Pro Football Hall of Fame in Canton, we're pretty big fans of football too. But Ohioans are also partial to other sports. Besides basketball, hockey, and soccer, we're big roller derby fans.

Not only is Canton the home of the Pro Football Hall of Fame, it's also the place where the NFL was founded.

*Welcome to*

# SPORTS

## 263 PRO FOOTBALL HALL OF FAME

**2121 George Halas Dr. NW, Canton, OH 44708; 330-456-8207**
**profootballhof.com**

For football fans, it's an emotional moment to stand in the Hall of Fame Gallery among the bronze busts of legendary players. That's only the beginning of the Hall of Fame experience, though. Many of the most iconic, historic times experienced by those Hall of Fame notables are chronicled in the Moments, Memories & Mementoes Gallery.

"A Game for Life," the hall's holographic theater, inspires fans with stories of Hall of Famers and the lessons for life to be found in football. The Lamont Hall Super Bowl Gallery and its Super Bowl Theater use interactive displays, film, and mementoes to call each Super Bowl game back to life. At a research-and-preservation center fans can find a carefully archived collection of rare documents and records. There are also exhibits devoted to officiating, and to other football leagues. Elsewhere in the museum, interactive video and trivia games entertain and test visitors' skills. Annual events held at the museum include the two-week Enshrinement Festival celebrating new inductees. Additionally, every year prior to the NFL season, a Hall of Fame exhibition game is played at Fawcett Stadium. At the continually evolving Hall of Fame Village, fans can find a concert venue, research facility, restaurants and shops, a Play Action Plaza, a water park, and a football-themed hotel. The Forever Lawn Complex maintains an eight-field facility for football, lacrosse, and soccer events.

## 264

### BASEBALL

### 264A Cincinnati Reds—Great American Ball Park

**100 Joe Nuxhall Way,**
**Cincinnati, OH 45202**
**888-729-4718**
**mlb.com/reds**

### 264B Cleveland Guardians—Progressive Field

**2401 Ontario Street,**
**Cleveland, OH 44115**
**216-420-4487**
**mlb.com/guardians**

### 264C Akron Rubber Ducks—Canal Park

**300 South Main Street,**
**Akron, OH 44308**
**330-253-5151**
**milb.com/akron**

### 264D Columbus Clippers—Huntington Park

**330 Huntington Park Lane,**
**Columbus, OH 43215;**
**614-462-5250 or**
**Ticket Line: 614-462-2757**
**milb.com/columbus**

### 264E Dayton Dragons—Day Air Ballpark

220 North Patterson Boulevard,
Dayton, OH 45402
937-228-2287
milb.com/dayton

### 264F Toledo Mud Hens—Fifth Third Field

406 Washington Street,
Toledo, OH 43604
419-725-4367
milb.com/toledo

### 264G Lake County Captains—Classic Auto Group Park

35300 Vine Street,
Willowick, OH 44095
440-975-8085
milb.com/lake-county

### 264H Lake Erie Crushers—Crushers Stadium

2009 Baseball Boulevard,
Avon, OH 44011
440-934-3636
lakereiecrushers.com

### 264I Mahoning Valley Scrappers—Eastwood Field

111 Eastwood Mall Boulevard,
Niles, OH 44446-1357;
330-505-0000
mlbdraftleague.com/mahoning-valley

## 265

## BASKETBALL

### 265A Cleveland Cavaliers—Rocket Mortgage Fieldhouse

One Center Court,
Cleveland, OH 44115
216-420-2000
nba.com/cavaliers

## 266

## FOOTBALL

### 266A Cincinnati Bengals—Paycor Stadium

One Paycor Stadium,
Cincinnati, OH 45202
513-621-3550
bengals.com

### 266B Cleveland Browns—Cleveland Browns Stadium

100 Alfred Lerner Way,
Cleveland, OH 44114
440-891-5000
Ticket line, 440-891-5050
clevelandbrowns.com
clevelandbrownsstadium.com

## 267

## HOCKEY

### 267A Columbus Blue Jackets—Nationwide Arena

200 West Nationwide Boulevard,
Columbus, OH 43215
614-246-2000
nhl.com/bluejackets

## 268

## ROLLER DERBY

These roller derby leagues meet in various locations. Visit their websites to find the dates, times, and locations of their games.

### 268A Akron Roller Derby, Akron

akronrollerderby.net

### 268B Burning River Roller Derby, Cleveland

burningriverderby.com

**268C** **Central Ohio Roller Derby, Mt. Vernon**

advkeen.co/central_ohio_roller_derby

**268D** **Cincinnati Rollergirls, Cincinnati**

cincinnatirollergirls.com

**268E** **Gem City Roller Derby, Dayton**

gemcityrollerderby.com

**268F** **Glass City Rollers, Toledo**

glasscityrollerderby.org

**268G** **Hell's Orchard Roller Derby League, Marietta**

wftda.org/leagues/helsorchard

**268H** **Little Steel Derby Girls, Youngstown**

wftda.org/leagues/little-steel

**268I** **Ohio Roller Derby, Columbus**

ohiorollerderby.com

**268J** **Southern Ohio Bruisers Roller Derby**

facebook.com/SouthernOhioBruisers

**269**

## SOCCER

**269A** **Columbus Crew—Historic Crew Stadium**

One Black & Gold Boulevard,
Columbus, OH 43211
614-447-4201
columbuscrew.com

**Football historian Jack Park has attended more than 400 games in Ohio Stadium and never misses a game against Ohio State's bitter rival, Michigan.**

# INDEX

## Y



## Z

# PHOTO CREDITS

Photos by Cathy Hester Seckman except as follows:

These images are used under CC 1.0 Universal (CC0 1.0) Public Domain Dedication, which can be found at creativecommons.org/publicdomain/zero/1.0/: **Warren LeMay:** 14, 17, 76

These images are used under Attribution 2.0 Generic (CC BY 2.0) license, which can be found at https://creativecommons.org/licenses/by/2.0/: **anyjazz65:** 43, no modifications, original image at flickr.com/photos/49024304@N00/3795831888/; **Doug Butchy:** 12, no modifications, original image at flickr.com/photos/dougbutchy/10584136425/; **Eric Drost:** 151, no modifications, original image at flickr.com/photos/edrost88/22318870620/, 169, no modifications, original image at flickr.com/photos/edrost88/53857992590/; **Jean Ogden Just Chaos Photography:** 150, no modifications, original image at flickr.com/photos/7326810@N08/53023733080/; **Paula R. Lively:** 52 (hot air balloons), no modifications, original image at flickr.com/photos/29621494@N02/3608658377/; **Sonja:** 55, no modifications, original image at flickr.com/photos/8308527@N02/4984013011/; **James St John:** 160 (flint), no modifications, original image at flickr.com/photos/jsjgeology/51432697525/; **Jeremy Thompson:** 56, no modifications, original image at flickr.com/photos/rollercoasterphilosophy/14882105085/; **Theresa Thompson:** 129, no modifications, original image at flickr.com/photos/theresasthompson/2744627705/

This image used under license from stock.adobe.com: **nasik:** 37 (GPS)

All images used under license from Shutterstock.com:
**4zevar:** 12 (masks); **aceshot1:** 32, 50, 82, 170; **Aeypix:** 101; **The American Explorer:** 46; **arthurgphotography:** 1 (Rock House), 142; **Jon Bilous:** 164; **BK Studio:** 173 (football); **Casey Fredette Media:** 122; **cjorgens:** 18; **Justin Lee DeLong:** 119; **Doclensoscope:** 73; **Dukesn:** 81 (bootlegger); **Matthew G Eddy:** 102; **Everett Collection:** 2; **Exporter:** 140 (wine bottle/glass); **Forde:** 4 (plane); **Zack Frank:** 86, 89; **Peter Hermes Furian:** 23 (Ohio map reference); **gladder:** 84, (Ohio flag reference); **Irina Gutyryak:** asphalt; **In-Finity:** 132 (presidential seal); **David Byron Keener:** 147; **Kenneth Keifer:** 31, 158; **Kevin Lush Photography:** 130; **Nicholas J Klein:** 157; **Jesse Kunert:** 74; **lizaakter:** 68 (tree); **LRYAPHOTOGRAPHY:** 6**6; David Majestic:** 94; **CHRISTOPHER MAMPE:** 118; **Marked Imagery:** xiv (MWCD); **Meda01:** 124 (Ohio); **Berry Medley:** 10; **Mike_O:** xiv (zipline); **murat irfan yalcin:** 26 (mussels); **NatureN8:** 20; **Aletkina Olga:** 34, (superman); **ONYXprj:** 58 (rollercoaster); **Sreekumar Pallath:** 112; **Elena Phoenix:** 138; **Photomike76:** 28; **Rajh.Photography:** 24; **rangizzz:** 152; **Red Light Media LLC:** 22; **Sailingstone Travel:** 116; **Ric Schafer:** 141; **SF photo:** 90; **Shidler3 Photos:** 65; **shriesik:** 70; **Kenneth Sponsler:** 1 (motorcycle), 9; **The Studio:** 144 (hiker); **Becky Swora:** 91; **Sylfida:** 115 (traffic light); **TimeLineArtist:** 160 *(Dunkleosteus terrelli)*; **uchenik:** 96 (cargo ship); **ultra designer:** 105 (cannon); **Kelly vanDellen:** 149; **Vejas:** 68 (Holden Arboretum); **VNWaltz:** 21; **Waqar421:** 137 (grad cap); **Wirestock Creators:** 97; **wisevectors:** 52 (twins)

## The Story of AdventureKEEN

We are an independent nature and outdoor activity publisher. Our founding dates back more than 40 years, guided then and now by our love of being in the woods and on the water, by our passion for reading and books, and by the sense of wonder and discovery made possible by spending time recreating outdoors in beautiful places.

It is our mission to share that wonder and fun with our readers, especially with those who haven't yet experienced all the physical and mental health benefits that nature and outdoor activity can bring.

In addition, we strive to teach about responsible recreation so that the natural resources and habitats we cherish and rely upon will be available for future generations.

We are a small team deeply rooted in the places where we live and work. We have been shaped by our communities of origin—primarily Birmingham, Alabama; Cincinnati, Ohio; and the northern suburbs of Minneapolis, Minnesota. Drawing on the decades of experience of our staff and our awareness of the industry, the marketplace, and the world at large, we have shaped a unique vision and mission for a company that serves our readers and authors.

**We hope to meet you out on the trail someday.**

**#bewellbeoutdoors**

# ABOUT THE AUTHOR

**Cathy Hester Seckman** is a lifelong resident of East Liverpool, Ohio, who has been a fan of day trips since her parents first said, "Let's take a ride!" on a Sunday afternoon. Writing this book has been an adventure, allowing her to discover new favorite places and revisit old ones.

Cathy is a an indexer and has compiled some 215 indexes. She has published more than a dozen short stories, hundreds of magazine articles, and thousands of newspaper articles. She is the author of *East Liverpool,* an Images of America title released by Arcadia Publishing in 2015. *Weirdo World,* her young adult fantasy novel, was published by Cool Well Press in 2012. As an indie author, she cowrote *Bad Moon Rising,* a murder mystery set between Woodstock and the Kent State shootings; *Too Many Secrets,* a women's fiction title; and an anthology, *$H_2O$ Mysteries.* Her most-recent novel, *Rightside/Wrongside,* was published by Wild Rose Press in 2023.